Entropic Affirmation

Entropic Affirmation

On the Origins of Conflict
in Change, Death, and Otherness

Apple Zefelius Igrek

LEXINGTON BOOKS

Lanham • Boulder • New York • London

Published by Lexington Books
An imprint of The Rowman & Littlefield Publishing Group, Inc.
4501 Forbes Boulevard, Suite 200, Lanham, Maryland 20706
www.rowman.com

Unit A, Whitacre Mews, 26-34 Stannary Street, London SE11 4AB

Copyright © 2018 by The Rowman & Littlefield Publishing Group, Inc.

British Library Cataloguing in Publication Information Available

Library of Congress Cataloging-in-Publication Data Available

LCCN 2018945969 | ISBN 9781498567992 (hardback : alk. paper) |
ISBN 9781498568005 (electronic)

♾™ The paper used in this publication meets the minimum requirements of American
National Standard for Information Sciences—Permanence of Paper for Printed Library
Materials, ANSI/NISO Z39.48-1992.

Printed in the United States of America

In Memory of Mariah Harvey, She Brought Joy to the World

Contents

Preface

The reason for writing this book is to develop a new methodological approach to radical, infinite otherness.[1] This new approach is necessary precisely because the traditional approaches are flawed in ways that cannot be rectified on their own. One such approach, familiar to anyone who has read Levinas, Derrida, or Irigrary, is to argue that greater openness and receptivity to infinite otherness is crucial to both ethics and politics. According to this line of thought, as we shall see in the ensuing chapters, it is precisely this receptivity which helps to mitigate and prevent the injustices that arise when we dissociate ourselves from the strange, inhuman, and incommensurable. But we shall also see that this influential approach is vulnerable to the critique that our relationship to what is infinite (or inhuman, incommensurable, etc.) cannot be measured in terms of greater or lesser openness; by definition whatever is infinite exceeds all such measurements equally. It is therefore inferred, in reference to a second traditional approach, that whatever is excessive in this way has no bearing on questions of justice or injustice. If all social values are equally exposed to what is infinite then there is no use in trying to distinguish them on this basis. And a third approach simply rejects the reality of infinite otherness altogether. If there is no validity to such a philosophical construct, then once again it will be inferred that it is both irrelevant and useless. But if it can be proven that what is infinite is both real and relevant, while nevertheless acknowledging that all of our social values are equally receptive to it, then it is incumbent upon us to elaborate what this means and how it is possible. What needs elaboration, then, is a methodological approach emphasizing the relevance of alterity and otherness to our social values without that relevance having anything to do with greater or lesser openness. This book therefore attempts to do just that by developing an alternative to the traditional methodological options.

The first chapter introduces the reader to the method that will guide the entire trajectory of this work—and that method is thanato-vitalism. As the name suggests, the method emphasizes the intimate connection between life and death insofar as the affirmation of one always includes the other. As will become clear throughout the following pages, the idea of the infinite which will serve as the basis of thanato-vitalism is most directly related to change and death. In this way, I am very much influenced by the likes of Heraclitus and Nietzsche in defending the view that nothing can be separated from the vicissitudes of boundless, primordial, incessant change. The method of thanato-vitalism is therefore distinguished from the second and third approaches to infinite otherness in its claim that the orientation of social values is indeed influenced by the fact that whatever we affirm necessarily includes such infinite aspects of change and death.[2] The second chapter highlights the heart of this method which is the concept of entropic affirmation. This is the concept that proves to us that the infinity of change and death is affirmed to the same degree in all social values, no matter what those values happen to be. Of course it may be debated whether or not there is indeed something infinite which is affirmed in all of our values to the same degree, and so I elaborate what I take to be the best arguments on behalf of this view. Assuming that these arguments are plausible, the third chapter explores the first consequence for social and cultural values that are said to be influenced by entropic affirmation. This first consequence is that we should no longer assert causal connections, no matter how rigid or loose, between the disavowal of otherness and the greater likelihood of catastrophe. All too often it is claimed (in the works of Baudrillard, Žižek, Butler, and so forth) that the disavowal of what is irreducible lends itself to war, violence, and catastrophe; but if the irreducible does in fact include an infinite dimension, as entropic affirmation suggests, then there are no greater or lesser modes of disavowal which could be distinguished as the basis of either peace or catastrophic violence. Any catastrophic trajectory relying on such logic must therefore be rejected.

While the third chapter explores a negative consequence of the present methodology (i.e., an observation that is critical of competing theories), the fourth begins to focus more explicitly on the nature of social values and social life as understood in the context of entropic affirmation. As already put forth, it is the view of this author that the unlimited aspect of change is affirmed in *all* social values—and to the same degree.[3] It follows, as I hope to show, that insofar as change is not only creative but also destructive, whatever we affirm necessarily includes this self-destructive tendency. This view is immediately contrasted with others, as we find with Foucault and Becker, suggesting that modern power regimes are focused solely on the optimization of life. This is an important debate to pursue further, as I write in chapter five that one of the primary inferences to be drawn from values that are both creative and destructive is that by their very nature they do not seek out complete integration with all other cultural and political modes of life. The debate, then, has to do with the proper analysis of the origins of conflict, and I contend that these origins have much more to do with the inherent ambivalence of these values rather than some kind of mythical construction which only ever emphasizes what is positive and life-enhancing. Between chapters four and five there is an interlude providing the reader with an application of the more ambivalent values—what I refer to as expansive singularities—to a variety of films exploring love, death, and the simulacrum. Although the interlude does not introduce a new concept to the main trajectory of thanato-vitalism, which is in fact why it is set aside as an interlude, it is nevertheless helpful in elucidating how the arguments of this trajectory can be applied to complex ethical and political issues raised by truly provocative films.

The sixth chapter continues to explore issues of change, death, and self-identity in relation to processes of sublimation. Although it is always preferable to pursue sublimation whenever it reduces the possibility of unnecessary conflicts, it is impossible to eradicate the consequences of our ambivalent values. Insofar as they embody entropic affirmation, which entails that they affirm their own singularity (i.e., a form of existence that ultimately disappears from this world), they will always introduce some form of division and antagonism into the larger social field. The seventh chapter fills out this logic in greater detail, proceeding step by step from concepts of time and teleology to entropic refraction and agonistic pathos. The conclusion of this argument is that while expansive singularities do seek out harmonious relationships with the world in which they exist, there must be some limit to this tendency if they likewise embrace the very antithesis of such expansiveness—that is, their own singularity. This particular chapter shifts in style compared to previous chapters in order to single out each of the conceptual steps that lead to this final conclusion. I would expect this to be helpful at some point in the book insofar as the overall methodological approach that has been developed here is irreducible to others which are more familiar to the reader. This also serves as my justification for adding a final chapter composed of questions and objections. Again, if I am right to think of the method contained within this book as irreducible to more traditional interpretations of otherness, then it is my responsibility to clarify as much as possible the sorts of questions that are likely to arise. While I cannot anticipate all such questions, it is my hope that in thinking through what I take to be the strongest possible objections I have made this theory of entropic affirmation more resilient, viable, and accurate.

NOTES

1. What is meant by infinite otherness is open to debate. For this reason it is associated with a network of terms that vary from author to author. These terms include the abyss, the outside, the incalculable, the secret, the trace, incommensurability, immanence, groundlessness, limitlessness, expenditure, and so on. I myself, for reasons given throughout this book, most closely associate the infinity of otherness with change and death.

2. As will be elaborated in later chapters change and death are associated with boundlessness in different ways: the first is infinite insofar as it inevitably overturns and permeates all boundaries, whereas the second is infinite in the sense that it is itself pure nothingness and therefore has no limits or boundaries at all.

3. This argument, along with several others, has been simplified for the purposes of this preface. It will of course be elaborated in much greater detail throughout the course of this work.

Acknowledgments

I would first like to thank the entire Philosophy Department at Oklahoma State University for all of their intellectual and moral support while I completed this project. I would also like to thank those professors of mine who encouraged original philosophical answers to seemingly intractable problems. This short list includes David Wood, Gregg Horowitz, Herbert Garelick, Virginia Held, Marx Wartofsky, James Miller, José Medina, Joan Stambaugh, Michael Taussig, William Franke, Michael Hodges, and John Lachs.

There are also several friends and colleagues who have inspired my research with thoughtful critiques and conversations. I therefore owe a very special thanks to Jason Wirth, Dylan McKee, Megan Burke, Cully Wiseman, Brian Kim, Elisabeth Calcaterra, Timothy Weidel, Eric Reitan, Libby Carlson, William Ricer, Mariah Harvey, Christopher Drohan, Lucienne Auz, Martin Ditto, and Keith Feldman.

Chapter 1

Thanato-Vitalism

When the reality of the infinite is embraced in ethics, cultural values, and political theory, the reason for doing so is connected to the claim that we should be more responsive to it.[1] So if it is said that there is something radical or infinite about our relations with the other, then we are not surprised when we are encouraged to be more open to these kinds of relations. But when this line of reasoning is rejected, it is often pointed out that what is infinite cannot be measured in terms of greater or lesser openness. And if there are no degrees of difference in this way, for the simple reason that infinity transcends all social relations equally, then such openness becomes irrelevant to our everyday decisions. On each side, of course, there are many significant differences of opinion. For the first group of thinkers it is far from settled what exactly is meant by the infinity or transcendence of the other. Irigaray writes, for example, that the identification of the other with God as defended by Levinas interferes with our respect for the other *as other* by subjecting our relations to a single mode of reason, spirit, and discourse.[2] And while the second group agrees in their rejection of absolute otherness as the starting point of ethics and politics, the true starting point remains uncertain. Eagleton reasons that it must have something to do with the body. We are humans, but we are no less animal for that. So given the fact that we are mortal and needy creatures, there is some hope that we can feel compassion for the suffering of others.[3] Badiou, however, argues that our determination to remain what we are is irreducible to the variegated flux of things: "To be sure, humanity is an animal species. It is mortal and predatory. But neither of these attributes can distinguish humanity within the world of the living."[4] Without a doubt, then, there are many such disagreements. But if we retain from the first group the insight that the infinite is relevant to the assessment of our values, while acknowledging the critique of the second group that greater or lesser

1

openness has nothing to do with it, then a new methodological approach will be required to articulate how exactly it remains relevant.

This approach begins with a concept of the infinite that extends beyond the realm of life, human or otherwise, even as it pervades it. In this way it is most closely associated with a principle of change that has no permanent limits or boundaries and thus cannot be defined in such terms. It is not reducible to what is other in the sense of a living person or animal, for that would imply that there is something in us that puts an end to change. If we keep to a strict interpretation of the infinite, then it is change that puts an end to us, and everything that we love and value, as opposed to the other way around. So what I have in mind is deeply influenced by how certain thinkers, in particular Bataille and Derrida, speak of absolute loss, immanence, the outside, the abyss, the supplement, expenditure, and so forth. Both of these writers can be interpreted as locating the infinity of the other as both inside and outside of ourselves. The former speaks of a realm of immanence in which every particle of existence exists in the world "like water in water."[5] In this realm useful distinctions have yet to be imposed on the flux of reality, so that it remains fluid and permeable. It is thus contrasted with the realm of tools which transforms whatever is in front of it into a series of discrete steps and purposes. As these steps and purposes serve what we need and desire, and are useful in this way, they are defined within a limited set of conditions. They are restricted according to this range of human activity. But for Bataille we can never entirely separate what is useful from what is useless, purposeless, and limitless. The deferral of means and ends that takes place through connecting one useful step to another must eventually terminate: "The absurdity of an endless deferral only justifies the equivalent absurdity of a true end, which would serve no purpose. What a 'true end' reintroduces is the continuous being, lost in the world like water is lost in water."[6] The true end, in our enjoyment of it, therefore ceases to be an end at all. We pursue one thing after another until we lose ourselves once more in the world without much sense of boundaries or limits. That of course doesn't imply that those limits are without any significance whatsoever. If we weren't invested in the aims and goals of our finite lives, then there would be nothing worth giving or sacrificing. The larger point, then, is that the infinity of change exceeds us. Whatever we delimit as an object or self-identical is temporary. And this kind of realization, which jolts us out of complacency, helps us to overturn structures of violence that seek nothing more than to exert power, control, and domination.[7]

This line of thought, both insightful and flawed, has been very influential.[8] Derrida draws directly from it when he discusses Bataille's concept of sovereignty, a concept closely related to loss and sacrifice: "Sovereignty provides the economy of reason with its element, its milieu, its unlimiting boundaries of non-sense. Far from suppressing the dialectical synthesis, it inscribes this synthesis and makes it function within the sacrifice of meaning. . . . For meaning, when lost to discourse, is absolutely destroyed and consumed."[9] It thus appears that this is not the kind of world in which we remain identical to ourselves. Everything that we do to preserve ourselves against boundless change is ultimately sacrificed to it. And if there is no foundation to things, if there is only change and difference in every direction, then the appropriate description for this would be an abyss. And this description has many implications for Derrida. It explains why all of our connections to the world are supplements, which is to say, modes of substitution in which we experience or represent something without it being fully present. So the fact that we do indeed interact with our surroundings in this way, as well as with ourselves and others, suggests that there is no fixed being—but only perpetual differences. Derrida makes this argument explicitly when he says that the supplement designates a form of textuality in an abyss.[10] While in this specific passage the abyss isn't specifically associated with anything beyond language (or with what I have thus far associated with the inside), if we look elsewhere it becomes clear that this is not a logocentric concept. Turning to his discussions of technology and prosthetics in either volume of *The Beast and the Sovereign*, the issue of self-division (and thus mortality) is raised precisely because of our relationship to a world that cannot be reduced to human limits and categories: "Everything that can happen to the *autos* is indissociable from what happens *in the world* through the prosthetization of an ipseity which at once divides that ipseity, dislocates it, and inscribes it outside itself *in the world*, the world being precisely what cannot be reduced here."[11] And this openness to change that operates both inside and outside of us, without any fixed boundaries, does have consequences. The assumption that we have no choice but to act according to instrumental calculations is what allows for the smooth functioning of injustice, whether it is economic, political, or otherwise.[12] So what needs to be done to resist this, at least in the context of Derrida's argument, is that we remain as open as possible to what is secret, other, and incalculable within each of us.

Not everybody agrees with this assessment, of course. Eagleton argues that the very nature of an incalculable kind of ethics is self-contradictory. If there are specific forms of responsibility, such as being loyal to my friends in times of need and hardship, then they cannot be derived from a state of affairs that is utterly ambiguous: "On this viewpoint, there are moral judgements, but they lack any sort of criteria or rational basis. There is no longer any relation, as there was for Aristotle or Marx, between the way the world is and how we ought to act within it, or between the way we are and what we ought to do."[13] There can be no such relation, according to this argument, when we are comparing something absolutely other to what is finite, social, and practical.[14] If we are expected to follow a moral code in life, it would be helpful if it could be formulated for us. Eagleton thus mocks the law of the other that imposes an unconditional demand upon us as "mysterious" for precisely the reason that it cannot have any relation to our lives. It can also be added that it doesn't make any difference whether we have in mind something transcendent, immanent, or both. If Eagleton's complaint focuses on the enigma of the other, Badiou reminds us that it can also be construed as trivial and commonplace: "Infinite alterity is quite simply *what there is*. Any experience at all is the infinite deployment of infinite differences. Even the apparently reflexive experience of myself is by no means the intuition of a unity but a labyrinth of differentiations."[15] In this way, then, acknowledging that the infinite other is immanent to each of us, and to all things, is one more strategy for making this concept seem insignificant. If all things manifest otherness, multiplicity, and self-differentiation to the same degree, then we cannot hope to make decisions on this basis. One set of values would have to be seen as equally heterogeneous as any other. So for this reason Badiou rejects the role of infinite alterity in his ethical and political views.[16] But if the infinity of change, death, and otherness remains relevant on a different basis, one which doesn't deny the equal embodiment of that infinity in all values and actions, then a new approach is needed to determine how this is possible.

Before going any further, however, it may prove helpful to say a few more things about what is meant here by change. The fundamental assumption with which I am working is that it is real, infinite, and absolute. This means, first of all, that change is not merely an illusion of the senses or the mind. It is what we experience happening every moment of our lives, and this experience is genuine. By contrast, there are other points of view that deny its reality in some way. One such denial stipulates that all things are fundamentally one.[17] If this is right, then change is an illusion in the sense that whatever is one with itself (and everything else) cannot change into that which it is not. If it is an all-pervasive, all-encompassing substance, then it cannot be transformed into something new, as that would imply that the original substance was not in fact all-encompassing. Any such imagined change would therefore be an illusion. But this is highly implausible. If there is an experience of change, even as an illusion, this experience cannot be reduced to oneness. The experience itself, as defined, would not be absolutely one with all things. It is the definition of an illusion that it diverges from reality, and thus the experience qua illusion would not be one with the truth. A similar problem arises for those views which state that what is eternal and self-identical is separate from the illusions of physical embodiment. This has been argued, for example, from the religious perspective that there is an immortal soul within each of us. But if change is relegated solely to the realm of matter and physical embodiment, then it is impossible to explain how the two realms are often conflated with one another. If the essence of the self is unchanging and eternal, then it can never take itself for anything else but what it is. But of course we identify with our bodies all the time. So in both cases, monistic and dualistic, it is difficult to explain how something that is pure, unchanging, and one with itself becomes something else entirely.

In the following chapters I will therefore presume that separating the world into two distinct and separate realms is a lost cause. Assuming that change is real it cannot be the case that it derives from an unchanging, self-identical foundation. This logic also applies to the relationship between nonidentity and the hypothesis that change proceeds by way of discrete units and elements. The experience of change as something that is happening during any given moment, so that such a moment fails to be one with itself, is already an indication that what is changing does not do so in a mechanistic fashion.[18] So it makes more sense to think of this process as something that is overflowing itself and therefore resistant to the fixed boundaries associated with discrete elements. And if there are no such fixed limits or boundaries, then we should stop thinking of change as being restricted to a finite portion of reality. However, it is possible to accept the above account of change as real, fluid, and limitless without furthermore accepting that it involves an absolute loss, as with the death of a friend. Rosi Braidotti makes this argument when she writes that the death of an individual is not the end of life but simply a new phase of it in which it reconnects with its ultimate source of vitality. What this source happens to be is a vibrant cosmic energy that does away with distinctions between life and death insofar as it is itself pure and absolute *zoe*: "Death is the ultimate transposition, though it is not final, as *zoe* carries on, relentlessly. Death is . . . the unproductive black hole that we all fear. Yet it is also a creative synthesis of flows, energies, and perpetual becoming."[19] The death drive, she continues with a fascinating twist, is therefore ultimately the desire to live more intensely. But if this is correct, then it becomes difficult to explain why exactly we fear death at all. If the answer is that we remain too narrowly focused on the survival of the ego, this merely resituates the question on another level—for we haven't yet explained why the ego wishes to survive when the experience of loss, on this model of change, should be felt and perceived as the reemergence of greater life forces. Braidotti writes that contrary to what we think on the conscious level, each of us desires to die in order to merge with the dynamic forces of life that are all around us. But if the process of aging and dying brings us closer to a more vibrant, more fulfilling source of energy then by definition there would be nothing in this process to engender a fearful response on the part of the ego. A more plausible explanation, then, is that our anxieties toward death are neither illusory nor myopic but grounded in the inexorable fact that it portends complete nothingness.

And once it is accepted that change is real, infinite, and absolute, it becomes impossible to say which of our values are more open to it than others. All social values impose a certain form on the world, but they fall equally short of doing this when being measured against that which exceeds all measurement. This also includes the nothingness of death insofar as it is defined by its absence of shape, form, and meaning. Of course, this doesn't stop us from trying to make some sense out of it, but the nothingness of death resists all efforts equally. In this way the concept of entropic affirmation, which is the concept that all values affirm change and death equally, is very closely aligned with Badiou's criticism apropos of radical otherness.[20] What distinguishes it from his line of thought, however, has to do with the way in which it continues to have relevance to our values despite the fact that this relevance has nothing to do with being more or less open to what is infinite. In this regard, it is important to keep in mind that even while the infinity of change and the nothingness of death exceed all human values and measurements equally, that doesn't preclude them from pervading those same values. Indeed, if only things outside of us underwent change, while we ourselves remained immune to its influences, then it would not in truth be infinite. This is also true of death: it may be that it transcends our best efforts to understand it, but insofar as we are mortal creatures we embody its absence in everything we do. And this fact has immediate implications for the orientation of our social values.

I will therefore argue that it is impossible to affirm anything at all separately from what is infinitely changing. It is valid, of course, that we are finite creatures plagued by finite thoughts, but there is nothing about this situation that restricts us to fixed parameters. On the contrary, everything that we love, desire, and affirm is itself an embodiment of the infinity which overturns all such restrictions. In this way, whatever it is that we value necessarily includes the destructive aspect of change and nothingness. And to the extent that what is life-affirming cannot be separated from this inherently destructive process, we will need to describe our social values and relations of power accordingly. It doesn't seem correct, then, to analyze bio-power and discipline primarily or solely in terms of life enhancement. If the premise of entropic affirmation is correct, which I hope to show in the next chapter, then every enhancement of life is bound up, either directly or indirectly, with its simultaneous destruction. One cannot be affirmed apart from the other. And in this way Foucault goes too far in his assessment when he argues that modern power dynamics are imbued with calculation "through and through."[21] It goes too far because it assumes that modern power dynamics seek only to optimize and enhance life as much as possible. It is quite true that these power dynamics cannot be reduced to a single, unified strategy or configuration. The unrelenting surveillance of the Panopticon is not equivalent to statistical models focused on birth and mortality rates. But in each case life is said to be controlled or coerced on behalf of optimizing its forces, aptitudes, and capabilities. Indeed, this is the reason why Foucault highlights the great paradox of modern power, which arises when we compare the life-enhancing tendencies of such power with the astonishing amounts of violent devastation witnessed in recent times. This would not be puzzling or paradoxical if it weren't for the fact that modern power and social values have been defined by Foucault and others (including Ernest Becker in *Escape from Evil*)[22] as being focused on "making live." If, however, Hal Foster is right that the life and death instincts are inseparable, such that what we desire is grounded in self-destructive change, then it becomes less plausible to contend that our motives can be framed simply in terms of life enhancement. In this light Foucault's paradox of power seems much less paradoxical, for if there is indeed a destructive aspect immanent to all social values and power relations then the fact that there are conflicts should no longer be viewed as inconsistent with those same values and relations. An explanation of our agonistic tendencies will therefore avoid this paradox altogether and instead make the assumption that it is our affirmation of change and otherness which should be highlighted.

Once this assumption has been made, it will eventually be discovered that it is precisely such an affirmation, along with its destructive tendency, which lends itself to the creation of social divisions. If all that we desired were nothing more than to integrate ourselves with the world around us, then such a possibility would be affirmed apart from infinite change. But if the limited and the unlimited are always bound together in all of our desires and social values, then we cannot prevent the affirmation of change from having certain destructive consequences. They will follow from the fact that it is this process of change itself which inevitably overturns its own limits and parameters. There is nothing fixed about it, so as soon as it takes on the form of a social need or value it is already putting into place the conditions for self-destructiveness. Of course, we also do what we can to preserve our way of life for as long as it seems worthwhile and viable. But this only goes so far since what is being preserved or optimized contains within itself a tendency toward self-dissolution. Once it is shown that it is our own values which affirm this tendency, an argument can be made that we do not desire full integration within the larger social field. The embodiment and affirmation of those values, in other words, necessitates the existence of other values which contest and potentially undermine our own. In this way social divisions cannot be avoided. If it is said in response that what is being established here is a false dichotomy between full integration and the rise of social divisions or cultural conflict, as it is possible to envision a multiplicity of coexisting values without those divisions, then what has been missed in this response is the fact that the self-destructive tendencies associated with our values are by definition harmful in some way.[23] I will thus conclude that what we affirm in our values, other than their vitality, is the existence of other values and ways of life in conflict with our own. Such a conclusion arises from the methodological approach of thanato-vitalism, an approach that begins with the insight that infinite otherness is indeed relevant to the orientation of our values—even if those values cannot be distinguished on the basis of being more or less open in relation to that otherness. If this insight proves to be correct, as I will attempt to show in more detail in the following pages, then it should compel us to rethink other analyses of power and conflict which fail to account for it.

NOTES

1. Obviously what is meant by either the infinite or absolute otherness varies with each author. I myself associate such terms with the kind of change that cannot be restricted by permanent limits, as will be seen in the following pages and chapters.

2. Luce Irigaray, *To Be Two*, trans. Monique M. Rhodes (New York: Routledge, 2001), 108.

3. Terry Eagleton, *After Theory* (New York: Basic Books, 2003), 155–56.

4. Alain Badiou, *Ethics: An Essay on the Understanding of Evil*, trans. Peter Hallward (London and New York: Verso, 2012), 11; Alain Badiou, *L'éthique: essai sur la conscience du mal* (Paris: Éditions Hatier, 1993), 13.

5. Georges Bataille, *Theory of Religion*, trans. Robert Hurley (New York: Zone Books, 1989), 19; Georges Bataille, *Théorie de la religion* (Paris: Éditions Gallimard, 1974), 27.

6. Bataille, *Theory of Religion*, 29; Bataille, *Théorie de la religion*, 38.

7. Bataille, *Theory of Religion*, 104; Bataille, *Théorie de la religion*, 137.

8. I accept the main premise that all limits are inevitably overturned, but it's difficult to see, as intimated earlier, what it means to be more or less complacent about this. If there is something limitless about immanence, then it would seem that every human value would embody it equally. So this is an argument to which I shall return in greater detail below, especially in the chapter on infinite embodiment.

9. Jacques Derrida, *Of Grammatology*, trans. Gayatri Chakravorty Spivak (Baltimore: Johns Hopkins University Press, 1976), 225; Jacques Derrida, *De la grammatologie* (Paris: Éditions de Minuit, 1967), 261.

10. Derrida, *Of Grammatology*, 163; Derrida, *De la grammatologie*, 225.

11. Jacques Derrida, *The Beast and the Sovereign, Vol. II*, trans. Geoff Bennington (Chicago: University of Chicago, 2011), 88; Jacques Derrida, *Séminaire: La bête et le souverain: 2002–2003* (Paris: Éditions Galilée, 2010), 138.

12. Jacques Derrida, *The Gift of Death*, trans. David Wills (Chicago: University of Chicago Press, 1995), 119; Jacques Derrida, *Donner la mort* (Paris: Éditions Galilée, 1999), 85–86.

13. Eagleton, *After Theory*, 153.

14. It's not clear, though, how Eagleton reconciles this argument with his views on death. He argues that the contingency and mortality of the body help us to establish a firmer foundation for ethics than what has been proposed by the likes of Derrida, Levinas, and Lyotard. But he also goes on to say that death is irreducible to cultural interpretations. So it is just as absolute as the other. Moreover, a close reading of these authors that he critiques should reveal a close connection between the finitude of our bodies and the infinity of the other. The dichotomy between one and the other is therefore misleading.

15. Badiou, *Ethics: An Essay on the Understanding of Evil*, 25–26; Badiou, *L'éthique: essai sur la conscience du mal*, 26.

16. While Badiou doesn't ignore the experience of otherness and difference considered in terms of an event, it is not the experience itself which has ethical implications for him. By contrast, the argument emphasized below will be that it is precisely the affirmation of otherness, regardless of openness or closure, that has such implications for us.

17. Many of these positions on change will be laid out in greater detail in the chapter on catastrophe. The primary goal of this particular chapter, however, is simply to present the methodology at work here in very broad terms. So my hope at this point is merely to provide the reader with a plausible starting point, even if this means delaying a more nuanced consideration of these ideas and arguments.

18. I take it that this is why a metaphysics of presence doesn't work, since every moment of identity or presence is simultaneously nonidentical and absent.

19. Rosi Braidotti, *The Posthuman* (Cambridge and Malden, MA: Polity Press, 2013), 131.

20. To reiterate the argument, if there is something that exceeds measurement in change as well as death, then all values are *equally* open to them. As I will show in the second chapter, this runs counter to those positions that attempt to distinguish values on the basis of how receptive they are to infinite otherness. But it should be added that this argument only applies to values and social constructs. It shouldn't be interpreted in the literal sense that each of us is equally healthy or sick. Regardless of how close to death I am in the literal sense, my values remain just as incommensurable with its nothingness as anyone else's.

21. Michel Foucault, *The History of Sexuality: An Introduction*, trans. Robert Hurley (New York: Vintage, 1990), 95; Michel Foucault, *Histoire de la sexualité: La volonté de savoir* (Paris: Editions Gallimard, 1976), 125.

22. Ernest Becker, *Escape from Evil* (New York: Free Press, 1975), 93–96.

23. This is not to suggest that all forms of agonistic social relationships are justified. It is in everyone's best interest to avoid forms of power that are derived from the scapegoating mechanism, for example. How the methodology of employed here helps us to avoid such unnecessary conflict will therefore be elaborated in subsequent chapters, in particular chapters 5 and 7.

Chapter 2

Infinite Embodiment and Entropic Affirmation

The first principle of this chapter, as well as my entire methodology, is that there are no permanent limits to nonidentity. Such a principle can be traced back as far as Heraclitus when he wrote of the earth melting into the sea, an everlasting fire burning through everything, and a river that never ceases to flow. These metaphors allude to a principle of nonidentity whereby the same, or what is delineated as familiar and known, is always pervaded with its other, that is to say, with the unfamiliar and unknown. Heraclitus's statement "I am as I am not" is best understood according to this principle that all things, including the identity of the self, are susceptible to their own dissolution, to their own incessant becoming and nonidentity.[1] This idea is also at work in Nietzsche's interrogations of the soul, the ego, religious ideals, eternal truths, and traditional moral views—all such views being thereby exposed as symptoms of decline and decadence. Throughout *The Flame of Eternity: An Interpretation of Nietzsche's Thought*, Krzysztof Michalski makes one of the strongest, most explicit arguments on behalf of this view: "In every moment of my life—to the extent that it is open to something heretofore alien, to something other, to a situation in which my concepts up to that point will fail me, as will my ability to assimilate what I encounter—my identity is once again placed under a question mark."[2] Identity, put another way, is never quite identical to itself, but is always open to the becoming of the world that places all of our ideals, limits, boundaries, and moral views under such a persistent question mark. In this chapter, however, it is not my intention to prove that the existential contours of identity are in fact pervaded in this way by forces of change, otherness, or nonidentity.[3] That issue is explored in several other locations throughout this book. But what I hope to do instead is overlay this fundamental premise with a new concept of affirmation, a concept that implies that we should no longer distinguish our cultural values

11

from one another on the basis of how responsive those values happen to be in relation to the principle of nonidentity.[4]

What is at stake here is the tendency on the part of a great number of writers, particularly in the continental tradition of philosophy, to categorize values and whole ways of life on the basis of whether they tend to be responsive to or shut off from what is irreducibly, irrevocably, absolutely other. A new concept of affirmation should put an end to this tendency, but it should do so without falling prey to the common fallacy of those who, by and large, repudiate the relevance of infinite otherness (or what has thus far been called nonidentity) to the concrete practice of everyday life.[5] My argument, then, is that a new approach to alterity is needed, one that, contrary to various pragmatic and hermeneutical critiques, embraces the relevance of radical alterity to the formation of our cultural values, but does so without promoting the post-phenomenological view that this relevance has to do with demarcating—no matter how loosely or rigidly—between ways of life that are totalizing and those that are not.[6]

Before proceeding, a few remarks on terminology will be useful in preventing unnecessary confusion. My central argument, as already stated, is that a new approach to nonidentity is needed. I myself use this term to say something about human experience, in particular, that it is always changing and that we may never fully retrieve or recuperate what has been lost to the movement of time. I also use this term in close proximity with other concepts—such as heterogeneity, otherness, expenditure, the trace, and the incommensurable. As these terms are used differently by a wide array of authors, my advice to the present reader is to keep in mind that I will have no choice, throughout this chapter and this book, but to shift back and forth between my own sense of these terms and how each of the other authors tend to use them. In several cases, in order to mitigate such confusion, I will revert to my own terminology to indicate that such a shift has taken place in the text. To this end, *infinite embodiment* should be understood as another way of describing the paradox of life in which we are always exposed to nonidentity and perpetual becoming.[7] This phrase, in itself, does not indicate anything new conceptually, but it is helpful in suggesting the direct link between concrete life and that which inexorably passes through it, which is to say, its inevitable destruction from both within and without. Furthermore, the concept of affirmation that will overlay what has thus far been described as both nonidentity and infinite embodiment is the concept of *entropic affirmation*. This is the concept that should provide us with a new approach to infinite embodiment, at least insofar as it implies that all cultural values are equally responsive to it.

A discussion of more traditional approaches to alterity in this chapter will help demarcate the way in which entropic affirmation sets itself apart from those approaches, while further discussions in the remaining chapters will elaborate the critical consequences that seem to follow once we take this concept as a methodological starting point for ethical and political inquiries.[8] To do this we must return to the concept of infinite embodiment to highlight what is so fascinating about it, whether it is viewed in terms of otherness, irreplaceability, becoming, or nonidentity.[9] As intimated above, the concept alludes to the fact that human experience, including human subjectivity as well as social organization, is never identical to itself. It is never one with itself, and it is never exactly equivalent to anything else either, for that would imply that nonidentity could be transformed into a category of rational understanding at odds with everything presupposed in the most radical theories of otherness. The assumption of deconstruction, to draw from one such theory, is that nonidentity always haunts and inhabits identity, for if this were not one of its founding premises, perhaps *the* founding premise, there would have to be definite limits to the work of deconstruction—there would have to be some things, like an eternal truth or autonomous subjectivity, that would necessarily be declared off limits to deconstruction. It is therefore no surprise that Derrida writes in *Paper Machine* that "one of the laws that deconstruction responds to, and that it starts off by registering, is that at the origin (thus the origin with no origin), there is nothing simple, but a composition, a contamination, the possibility at least of grafting and repetition."[10]

To say that there is nothing simple is to reiterate the basic assumption addressed at the beginning of this chapter, namely, that there are no permanent limits to change, multiplicity, or nonidentity. Whatever seems simple or straightforward, according to this "law" of deconstruction, is already slipping away from our all-too-human comprehension of things, from our limited, perspectival, contaminated view of the world. To those who have been hostile toward deconstruction, this kind of formulation strikes them as pretentiously self-contradictory. To this objection Etienne Balibar provides us with a classic response, namely, that "it simply ignores that the element of contradiction did not derive primarily from an intellectual decision to ignore the rules of logic, but from a deep understanding of the aporetic character of the experience itself."[11] It is experience as such, then, that is so fascinating in its inexorable tendency to overflow itself, to contradict and destroy its own limits, to resist being caged up by the same laws of human identity that are themselves uncontrollably sinking away into the infinite sea of nothingness rendered so poetically by Heraclitus.

This aporetic character of experience informs all of Derrida's work. It doesn't matter if the theme has to do with forgiveness, mortality, technology, or language, in every case there is an aporetic dimension of the problem that must be addressed. This dimension remains irreducible to conditional beliefs or desires, precisely insofar as it presupposes *both* the conditional as well as the unconditional. That is to say, there is a fundamental aspect of experience that reveals our empirical, conditional, and pragmatic tendencies, but there is simultaneously another aspect of experience that is pervaded with something unconditional—not in the sense that it stands apart from time or change, but in the more radical sense that it is never one with itself and therefore exceeds all reductions to predetermined conditions and parameters. For those who are familiar with Derrida's thinking, it is needless to say that the two aspects are inextricably bound up with one another, so much so that he calls them indissociable: "These two poles, *the unconditional and the conditional*, are absolutely heterogeneous, and must remain irreducible to one another. They are nonetheless indissociable."[12] This quote lays out the aporia in unmistakable fashion: the two poles are both heterogeneous and indissociable. The same and the other, the conditional and the unconditional, the possible and the impossible—these poles of experience are bound together in a way that can never be conveyed in terms of a rational or normalizing explanation.

Such an explanation would translate the unconditional abyss of experience into something known and familiar, into something that can be mastered and controlled, but of course then it would no longer make sense to think of that aspect of experience as something truly heterogeneous. In reference to Bataille's work on sovereignty, Derrida describes this operation as "totally other" even as it never escapes or transcends Hegelian dialectics.[13] So the aporetic dimension is now described less in terms of the conditional and the unconditional than by reference to the operations of sovereignty and lordship (*la maîtrise* in the original, thus underscoring not only Hegel's sense of social hierarchy but also skill, mastery, and control), but the deconstructive implications are the same. Bataille's notion of sovereignty mustn't be confused, Derrida writes, with a simple, naïve return to innocence or play without rules, for that would represent an abstract immediacy all too easily reabsorbed into Hegel's phenomenological system: "The transgression of meaning is not an access to the immediate and indeterminate *identity* of nonmeaning, nor is it an access to the possibility of *maintaining* nonmeaning."[14] Whether characterized as play or systematic dialectics, pure self-identity is never an option: the sovereign operation of risk, chance, and expenditure is never identical to itself, but always torn asunder by the infinite groundlessness of life and our normalizing, pragmatic, anthropocentric attempts to nevertheless feel at home in the world.[15]

It should go without saying that not everyone agrees with this formulation of the aporetic quality of experience. Not everyone draws from the language of deconstruction or sovereignty. But I will expand upon these initial ideas and insights in order to expose what I believe to be a common line of thought that is plagued by a common kind of fallacy—regardless of the theoretical language being used. This line of thought begins, as I have already written, with a concept of nonidentity that belongs to a constellation of terms including sovereignty, expenditure, immanence, incommensurability, and singularity.[16] What is being gestured toward by this constellation of terms, certainly in the works of Bataille and Derrida, has to do with a notion of experience that cannot be reduced to our typical categories of either rational or ethical normativity. Understandably, then, there is no single formulation to express the ways in which embodied experience perpetually slips away from itself. There is no magical word or argument that will shed light, once and for all, on what is happening to us when we perceive that there is something within perception that cannot be trapped, limited, or confined to that same perception. Bataille therefore describes this experience with a variety of poetic and theoretical formulations, often times within the same book, as can be recounted throughout *Inner Experience* where he writes that such an experience puts everything under question, that it is its own goal, that it represents no longer wanting to be God, that it overturns instrumental rationality, and that it is also a movement of energy that streams outwardly into a vortex of immeasurable agitation: "Your life is not limited to that ungraspable inner streaming; it streams to the outside as well and opens itself incessantly to what flows out or surges forth towards it."[17]

What is being called to our attention is the plain fact that we are never isolated, that human experience is a constant streaming of overflowing forces and energies never to be confined to permanent boundaries. For those of us who are influenced by the likes of Heraclitus or Nietzsche, this kind of formulation apropos of change is going to be attractive. But a significant problem arises when it is used to distinguish closed systems from open systems, restrictive economies from general economies. And this is undoubtedly what Bataille does when he writes that certain forms of dogma, such as the belief in God or immortality, create an obstacle to the streaming flux of life that is all around us. While he does not argue that a closed, restrictive economy is one that ultimately puts a stop to such overflowing impermanence, as that would be impossible by his own metaphysical assumptions, he nonetheless maintains a certain conceptual distinction between social systems on the basis of how restrictive they are in relation to that streaming flux. The concept of entropic affirmation, by contrast, stipulates that all such distinctions are false. They must be false insofar as Bataille and others posit an ungraspable, uncontainable, irreducible aspect of human experience, for it is such a fundamental aspect of experience—labeled unconditional by Derrida—that makes it impossible for us to categorize any value system as less open than another in relation to what is infinitely irreducible.

The previous claim needs further elaboration, and doing that requires that we continually attend to how these two systems, restrictive and general, tend to be contrasted with one another.[18] In the first, what is excessive, exuberant, and contingent is subordinated to what is known and familiar. The infinite movement of change becomes for us something predictable and recognizable so that we no longer feel that our lives are inherently meaningless. In the second, by contrast, the unknown takes precedence. This doesn't mean that we have immediate access to some "beyond," or that we can entirely overthrow our instrumental needs and values, but for Bataille everything that we oppose to the heterogeneity of life will ultimately be overturned, which in turn reveals the ineradicable, inexorable movement of nothingness at the heart of everything that we love and embrace: "Life will dissolve itself in death, rivers in the sea, and the known in the unknown. Knowledge is access to the unknown. Nonsense is the outcome of every possible sense."[19] The distinction between the two systems, then, is that the first disavows this relation between life and death, the known and the unknown, whereas the second remains open to it. This isn't a sharp distinction, but it is a distinction nonetheless, without which there would be no need for exposing the diverse methods of disavowal prevalent today in politics, religion, and social life in general.

Derrida affirms this approach when he writes that Bataille's sovereignty, far from excluding the importance of either knowledge or meaning, puts them in relation to a movement of *non-savoir* that ultimately exceeds them: "The writing of sovereignty places discourse *in relation* to absolute non-discourse. Like general economy, it is not the loss of meaning, but, as we have just read, the 'relation to this loss of meaning.' It opens the question of meaning. It does not describe unknowledge, for this is impossible, but only the effect of unknowledge."[20] We do not have access to anything like sovereignty, death, nonidentity, or non-discourse considered in themselves, as if it were possible for us to experience a mystical unknown set apart from what we categorize as known. But at the same time, we are always necessarily exposed to what tears us apart from within, to the boundless streaming of life into something hauntingly dark and obscure, so that every opposition between the inside and the outside, the self and the other, remains vulnerable to a process of deconstruction that takes place with or without our consent. Derrida reaffirms this vulnerability when he writes in *Psyche: Inventions of the Other* that a certain orientation toward death sets everything in motion "toward the beyond of all closed systems."[21] There is always a risk of simplifying when thinking through the distinction between open and closed systems, but for the purposes of the current analysis it seems clear that for these two writers, Bataille and Derrida, any system that tends to repudiate its intrinsic permeability, by creating myths of God-like immortality or distracting us with vapid consumerism, will be contrasted with systems that are more open to change and otherness.

While this distinction seems plausible, I will continue to argue that it is false. Assuming that there is something infinitely elusive within ourselves, within all of our embodied experiences, is to suggest that every experience, every perception, and every social system of values will fall *equally* short of revealing its "essence." If we accept the first principle of infinite embodiment, whereby it is acknowledged that finite creatures such as ourselves are exposed in everything we do and think to an experience of presence intimately bound up with its own absence, with a process of dissolution that eats away at us at all times, then we are compelled to agree that a so-called restrictive economy is no further removed from this indeterminacy than a general economy. Before elaborating this view in greater detail, it may be useful to summarize it in its most concise form using terminology that is freed up from the typical deconstructive trajectories.[22] As already noted, the concept of infinite embodiment does not in itself capture anything new about experience that hasn't been said before in terms of alterity, nonidentity, the sublime, or the aporetic. These terms, and many others discussed above and below, cannot be said to be interchangeable. But they do hint at something that can be called incommensurable in human experience, namely, the way in which experience itself is irreducible to reifying social practices. The concept of infinite embodiment reinforces that same irreducibility, but is moreover suggestive of the concretely lived paradox in which embodied finitude is continually exposed to that which it will never fully grasp or understand, namely, its own disappearance. The argument that I will elaborate, defend, and reinforce in the following pages, then, can be briefly stated as follows: *infinite embodiment implies entropic embodiment and entropic embodiment implies entropic affirmation.* The first idea of this argument, that we are always exposed to infinite change and absolute death, has been defended elsewhere.[23] So I will not repeat myself here.[24] Furthermore, the task of the present chapter is not to provide such a defense, but to explore the possibility of drawing new insights from this metaphysical starting point.

And such a possibility begins with the transition from the first idea to the second idea, in which it is stated that infinite embodiment implies entropic embodiment. To the extent that finite life continually undergoes change, so that it is never identical to itself at any given moment, it follows that this form of life is mortal rather than immortal—hence the term entropic embodiment. This first step, however, is not likely to generate much controversy. One should expect more resistance to the transition that takes place between the second and third ideas, as it is not immediately clear that we all affirm entropic embodiment equally.[25] While the full explanation for this step will take some time, at this point we can at least gesture toward the basic thought process according to which the principle of entropic embodiment is continually reinforced in all of our values. As these values are never affirmed outside of their own concrete temporality, this line of thought suggests that what *is* affirmed is nothing more absolute or eternal than the embodiment of the values themselves. All values, inasmuch as they are consistent, affirm themselves—which in turn implies that they affirm their own groundlessness, their own embodied decay and degeneration. And since this groundlessness is infinite, as stipulated in the idea of infinite embodiment, we cannot say which values embody it more than others. There are no means of deciding the issue when the infinity of change (or the nothingness of death) exceeds all of our values equally. In this way the groundlessness embodied in those values also transcends them, simply by virtue of the fact that what is infinite pervades everything even as it is reducible to nothing. So every human value both affirms and rejects its own groundlessness equally. If this is right, then entropic affirmation suggests that we give up the theoretical distinction between values that suppress the alterity of experience and other values, referred to in several theories of "infinite responsibility," that are described as more responsive and more open to it.

Following this logic to its conclusion, we must abandon any argument suggesting it is possible for some values to be more open than others to what is infinitely elusive. Whether such a distinction is stated in terms of immanence or transcendence does not change the fact that all values and actions stand in the same disproportionate relationship to that which infinitely exceeds them. By contrast, in the case of specific demands and duties, we know what is expected of us because there is nothing inherently paradoxical in formulating such principles. But if we have in mind something "infinitely demanding," as Critchley puts it, then we deprive ourselves of knowing what this means. To the extent that every finite formulation of ethics stands in the same relationship to what is infinite and unconditional, at least insofar as the relationship itself is incommensurable, then we will need to rethink ethics without recourse to anything akin to infinite responsibility.[26] At this point it would be impossible to respond adequately to objections before laying out the argument more fully in all of its ramifications, but ignoring them creates an impression that the project could be sabotaged from the beginning. In hopes of allaying this fear, I will respond to one objection that now seems germane with the caveat that it will be more fully addressed as my argument continues to be developed. First of all, it may appear that I have constructed a straw man critique. I contend that it is impossible to demarcate between closed and open social systems on the basis of how attentive they are to what is infinitely elusive as all such systems remain equally open to it.[27] However, it may be said that nobody actually draws this distinction. Nobody does this because it is acknowledged that an ethics of infinite responsibility, as Kelly Oliver puts forth, is simply an ideal.[28] There are no social practices that can be properly described as having attained this ideal, but they should nevertheless be distinguished from totalizing practices insofar as the latter tend to rein-force processes of exclusion, oppression, and dehumanization. But labelling infinite responsibility as an ideal doesn't help us to avoid the plain fact that if there is something immeasurable about it, then we still lack the means of discerning which social practices are more attentive to it than others. This is a simple point, but it is easy enough to forget when comparing specific kinds of dispositions and attitudes. Hence, when Michael Sandel argues throughout his *Case against Perfection* that we should replace our drive to mastery with the values of humility and sympathy, he appeals to our intuition that some moral dispositions and attitudes are more open than others to the inherent dis-sonance of life. In this way he draws a close connection between such moral attitudes and his entire discussion of the unbidden:

> In a social world that prizes mastery and control, parenthood is a school for humility. That we care deeply about our children, and yet cannot choose the kind we want, teaches parents to be open to the unbidden. Such openness is a disposition worth affirming, not only within families but in the wider world as well. It invites us to abide the unexpected, to live with dissonance, to reign in the impulse to control.[29]

Intuitively, it is difficult to deny that humility seems like the kind of moral attitude that would teach us "to be open to the unbidden." But if what we have in mind is a *general* sense of the unbidden, rather than something in particular, then the intuition must be false. While it is entirely possible for someone to be more open than another person in relation to a particular set of conditions—from meeting people and reading books to traveling, danc-ing, and drinking—there is no reason to think this must be true in the case of what is metaphysically unbidden. Insofar as the given nature of the world, in terms of its fundamental contingency, lacks either meaning or purpose, it simply doesn't make sense to describe one set of values or attitudes rather than another as better approximations of what the world calls for—because an indifferent, purposeless world doesn't call for anything. Whether we are humble or arrogant, apathetic or generous, all of our values and actions reflect the unbidden nature of the world equally.

This particular critique of Sandel stems directly from the idea of entropic affirmation, which thus far has been stated in a few different ways: (1) all values are equally exposed to (and removed from) that which is deemed to be infinitely incommensurable; (2) all values equally affirm their own embodied groundlessness; and (3) all values equally reflect the purposeless contingency of the world. All of these formulations reiterate the same entropic argument that what we affirm must always be open to change and absolute loss, for it is impossible to separate anything affirmed or valued in this world apart from its own temporality and destruction. The critique of Sandel and others follows from this argument because it precludes the possibility of some values, such as humility or kindness, from being more open than others to what exceeds all comprehension. If we think of the absolute loss of death, for example, it is impossible to say which values are more open to it than others when all of them are equally transcended by its infinite meaninglessness. Of course, if it were more accurate to say that death contains a hidden truth, that it is perhaps a passageway from this world to an imperishable one, then we could define and compare values in relation to that deeper meaning. If we admit, however, that death is real, that all values belong to a finite shape of time that is perpetually slipping away into emptiness, then we will have to make the argument that those values never affirm anything beyond that relationship to death. This view is unusual for many reasons. Perhaps what makes it most unusual is that it rejects the common assumption that there are many examples of values and beliefs that refuse to acknowledge the sad reality of human mortality. The religious belief in the afterlife has often been cited in this way since it seems obvious, at least from an atheistic perspective, that the proponents of immortality have deluded themselves with a pleasant, reassuring dream.[30] In relation to the entropic argument three things can be said in response to this common assumption:

First, although the belief in eternal life may be real, the desire for it is not. This follows from what was said above about the embodiment of values in relation to change and death. In each case those values embody their own dissolution since there is nothing in this world that can be set apart from what is always changing. So it is not as if what destroys us and our values only does so from the outside. Our desires and values are themselves the manifestation of change that works against those same desires and values. And if these values necessarily bring about their own death and destruction, then it must be inferred that they only affirm life by also affirming death. I am therefore in agreement with Hal Foster's observation that all instincts are intimately bound up with the death drive.[31] As this is an important point, it will require further elaboration in later chapters. Second, while the belief in everlasting life constitutes a denial of death, this denial is no stronger in the case of religious beliefs as compared to secular ones.[32] Such a denial is just one way of rejecting life's underlying emptiness. Death, for us, is an especially poignant and stirring manifestation of this emptiness, and so it is no surprise that we do what we can to construct values that provide us with a sense of hope and meaning—no matter how absurd or tentative. But as to which of these values more strongly represses the underlying void of everything, it is impossible to make comparisons when even the slightest sense of hope, or even the most delicate gesture toward meaning, implies a contradiction with the meaninglessness associated with death. If the phenomenon of death, in other words, culminates in the destruction of all shape and form, as with the constructs of human values, then the idea that some of these values are more closely aligned with it than others is implausible. Whatever shape or form of meaning that we attribute to the infinitely elusive nature of death is equally as mythical as any other. And third, if we keep in mind this infinite aspect of change and death (since the former is never-ending and the latter transcends shape and form), it follows that we lack all means of distinguishing our values in relationship to it, *for what is infinite cannot be used to measure what is finite, limited, or conditional.*[33] So we must give up the project of determining which values and attitudes are more open to death than others, as all of them exist in the same disproportionate relationship to unconditional loss. Since everything we say and do exposes us to something infinite within us, we cannot make distinctions on this basis. It is therefore incorrect to presume that the believer in immortal life, whether the life of the soul or something more cosmic and boundless, affirms death any less than the atheist, for in both cases the two individuals have committed themselves to the kinds of values, concrete and embodied, that are themselves equivalent to an infinite movement of loss that must be affirmed as soon as anything is affirmed.[34]

It is possible to view this movement of loss in a less disquieting manner. What I have suggested above is that the construction of any value presupposes a certain limit, a certain frame of existence, that is equally exposed to and removed from that which transcends all such limits. And to the extent that these limits provide us with a particular sense of hope and meaning, depending upon one's values, we are bound to reject, in some fashion or other, the meaninglessness of our lives.[35] This meaninglessness, however, remains at the vanishing point of all values, and thus it continues to haunt us. By contrast, Irigaray's interpretation of death and becoming is much more positive. She acknowledges limits, without which the self and the other are fused, but these limits do not imply grief or suffering.[36] On her view, the underlying reality of change has less to do with an abyss of nothingness than with the beauty, harmony, and blossoming of what gives birth to us: "In reality, the tempest belongs to an ensemble composed not of violence but of harmony. Nevertheless, Western man chooses to measure himself against the terrible rather than the calm. He remembers the frightening aspect of nature and forgets its mild sweetness."[37] But if nature is fundamentally peaceful, whence the belief that within it lurks something violent, dark, and abysmal? For Irigaray, this is simply the result of projection: "Recognizing the irreducible difference of the other opens an abyss in consciousness, in knowledge, in truth. It seems that man chooses to ignore this irreducible difference, preferring instead to perceive and project this abyss onto the cosmic."[38] The abyss that "devours and engulfs" us is therefore based on a misconception, one that has been confused with the irreducible difference of the other.[39] But if change is both infinite and absolute, it is difficult to know how it is that we avoid being subsumed within it. If death is absolutely final, such that our physical embodiment and awareness completely disappear, it would seem appropriate to refer to this negation of presence as something abysmal and fathomless, precisely due to the fact that it exceeds our finite limitations. Nevertheless, it might be that the *feeling* of loss can be avoided if we refrain from trying to be possessive: "Perceiving you does not involve losing me or you, as long as I accept that this perception is not simply mine. It is mine and not mine."[40] It is mine and not mine, Irigaray continues, because it unites us without thereby implying that the other is an object or possession.

While this is absolutely correct, it's not clear why this precludes loss in the tragic sense. To the extent that I either value or love someone, the ordinary way of interpreting my feelings is by saying that I would like for the other person to do well in life: to be happy, healthy, and so forth. By definition, then, the absence of such things is disappointing. So one paradox of entropic affirmation is that we cannot affirm any value without likewise affirming its loss: life is directly and intimately bound up with death and thus to affirm one is to affirm the other. There are thus two basic conclusions to end this chapter. First, as I argued earlier, it is impossible that some values affirm the absoluteness of death any more or any less than others. They affirm it equally as there are no means of quantitative or qualitative measurement. And second, as I have tried to show in response to Irigaray, it is impossible that our values circumvent this affirmation of loss: to like or love anything at all is to invest ourselves in its flourishing and thus to affirm what cannot be separated from it, namely, loss, absence, and emptiness. That's not to say that we all affirm loss in the same exact way. I have made the assumption in this chapter that our relation to the infinite is equal insofar as it exceeds all of our values to the same degree, but there are of course specific differences in how we respond to change and death that *can* be measured and compared, whether this has to do with ritual, emotion, socialization, anxiety, happiness, or whatever else. But in each case there is always the affirmation of loss—and this loss includes the loss of whatever we value and love. Hence the tragic dimension cannot be avoided; we affirm loss and flourishing at the same time as we affirm anything. But thus far I have only drawn inferences from an assumption about change that not everyone will accept, an assumption that it is infinite and absolute. In the next chapter it will therefore be incumbent upon me to elaborate a few reasons on behalf of this interpretation, and I will do so in response to theories suggesting that our relation to irreducible change and otherness should be modified in an effort to avoid catastrophic social tendencies.

NOTES

1. Heraclitus, *Fragments: The Collected Wisdom of Heraclitus*, trans. Brooks Haxton (New York: Viking, 2001), 51.

2. Krzysztof Michalski, *The Flame of Eternity: An Interpretation of Nietzsche's Thought* (Princeton, NJ: Princeton University Press, 2012), 53.

3. So in this chapter my aim is simply to explore the theoretical consequences of this assumption without providing an original argument on its behalf. Nevertheless, in the ensuing chapters there will be opportunities for revisiting this assumption and elaborating its finer points when necessary.

4. Although we want to be precise, we should not let ourselves get hung up on inflexible jargon. So, what I mean here by nonidentity, for the purposes of my analysis, will be connected to other related ideas—including alterity, otherness, heterogeneity, becoming, *différance*, the impossible, the trace, and so forth. All of these terms have different meanings when used by a wide variety of authors, but in my analysis they form a constellation of ideas having mainly to do with the experience of change (and loss) being irreducible to permanent structures of identity.

5. It is not unusual to critique writers for their treatment of otherness as an inaccessible reality, from which it is concluded that we should formulate our values in more pragmatic, everyday terms. I will return to that critique by the end of the next chapter. In the meantime I simply want to clarify that even though I agree that we cannot distinguish our values by how open they are to infinite otherness, I will nonetheless maintain, unlike the diacritical or pragmatic critiques, that the unlimited range of nonidentity does in fact make a difference in how we construct those values.

6. What was said earlier about values being more or less responsive than others to nonidentity should be kept in mind here, so that what is totalizing refers to a way of life (or system of values) that is said to be *less* responsive to this nonidentity. It is precisely this distinction that I will reject.

7. The paradox is that we are finite creatures exposed to something infinite that moves through us and beyond us, as with the radical otherness of becoming.

8. The concept and the methodology are obviously going to be closely conjoined. More will have to be said about the methodology, however, once the concept of entropic affirmation is elaborated in greater detail, as the latter helps to establish the contours and the trajectory of the former. What can be said at this early stage is merely that the critical consequences to be elaborated in this book will have mainly to do with a critique of how traditional approaches to otherness have used that concept of otherness as a way of deconstructing systems of totality. This book, then, exemplifies a critique of those approaches from the perspective of entropic affirmation, while a more positive unfolding of this concept and method in relation to cultural values will have to await a second book.

9. I must add one more caveat before continuing. A crucial difference between my view of alterity and that of thinkers similar to Levinas and Irigaray is that mine relates primarily to change and loss, in a primordial sense, while their focus is defined by intersubjective ethics. While these two categories are not mutually exclusive,

prioritizing one dimension over the other will have consequences. But no matter how one conceives of radical difference and alterity, my critique will be applied in a consistent fashion by rejecting any ethical position that attempts to portray some values and attitudes as more open than others to *whatever* is taken to be infinite.

10. Jacques Derrida, *Paper Machine*, trans. Rachel Bowlby (Stanford, CA: Stanford University Press, 2005), 139.

11. Etienne Balibar, "Derrida and the 'Aporia of the Community,'" *Philosophy Today* 53, no. Supplement (2009): 8.

12. Jacques Derrida, *On Cosmopolitanism and Forgiveness*, trans. Mark Dooley and Michael Hughes (London and New York: Routledge, 2001), 44.

13. Jacques Derrida, *Writing and Difference*, trans. Alan Bass (Chicago: University of Chicago Press, 1978), 260; Jacques Derrida, *L'écriture et la différence* (Paris: Éditions du Seuil, 1967), 382.

14. Jacques Derrida, *Writing and Difference*, 268; Jacques Derrida, *L'écriture et la différence*, 393.

15. Although Camus uses a markedly different language than that of Derrida, we observe nearly the same logic of incommensurability in his concept of the absurd when he writes that the indifference of the world to human aims and projects can never be overcome. Albert Camus, *The Myth of Sisyphus, and Other Essays*, trans. Justin O'Brien (New York: Knopf, 1955).

16. It is true, as mentioned in the first few sentences of this chapter, that the methodology of the present work likewise begins with this concept of nonidentity (i.e., infinite embodiment). The critique that will shortly follow, then, is not a critique of the concept but of its common appropriation for distinguishing closed social systems from others that are typically described as being open, sovereign, responsive, loving, or hospitable—depending upon the nomenclature of the writer.

17. Georges Bataille, *Inner Experience*, trans. Leslie Anne Boldt (Albany: State University of New York Press, 1988), 94; Georges Bataille, *L'expérience intérieure* (Paris: Éditions Gallimard, 1943), 111.

18. Perhaps it is also useful to remind the reader that this vocabulary will not be carried forward throughout the entire chapter or book. The contrast between what is restrictive and general will be described and written about differently by other writers who may not have much else in common with Bataille other than the attempt to open up a space of experience irreducible to totalizing systems of control, an attempt that I will counter as misguided regardless of the writer under discussion—misguided insofar as all systems are *equally* open to this experience.

19. Ibid., 101/119.

20. Derrida, *Writing and Difference*, 270; Derrida, *L'écriture et la différence*, 397.

21. Jacques Derrida, *Psyche: Inventions of the Other* (Stanford, CA: Stanford University Press, 2007), 283.

22. What I have in mind here is the familiar way in which an acknowledgement of radical otherness lends itself to various critiques of totality, the simulacrum, acceleration, dogmatism, techno-idealism, and so forth. Once it is accepted that the indeterminacy of embodied experience does not justify such political critiques, we will be forced to forge ahead in a new theoretical direction.

23. It is defended most explicitly in those sections where I consider the possibility that change is either illusory or finite. This is done briefly in the introductory chapter on thanato-vitalism and in more detail in the following one on the catastrophic trajectory. It might also be said that it is defended implicitly whenever related ideas appear, as with Derrida's supplement or Butler's discussions on mourning and loss.

24. Although I would like to add that Michalski gives one of the strongest formulations of this view in his critical engagement with Nietzsche. He contends in *The Flame of Eternity* that if there is any experience of change or rupture in this world, then that change says something about the rest of reality. What it says is that there are no eternal truths, the kind of truths that structure all of reality, for if they truly existed then I would not experience myself at this moment as lacking in any way. Michalski, 53.

25. This is another way of expressing the central idea of entropic affirmation. As stated earlier, the new approach to alterity will do away with the distinction between closed and open systems, between values that seem to repress or assimilate otherness and values that tend to be more responsive to it. Hence, if this distinction is rejected, it will have to be concluded that we all affirm nonidentity, including its entropic embodiment, equally.

26. And if we undertake such a project without giving up the relevance of what is infinitely elusive to the creation of values, then we will need a new methodology for doing this. This methodology will not ignore the relevance of radical alterity in how we think about our values, but neither will it resort to the usual way of understanding this relevance in terms of distinguishing open from closed economies.

27. It may seem strange to say, in the same paragraph, that all systems fall short of the immeasurable while also remaining equally responsive to it. But there is no contradiction as long as we think of the infinite in a manner that includes the finite. Accordingly, it both exceeds *and* pervades finite social systems. Hence, it cannot be effectively argued that any social values are more attentive than others to the immeasurable when, by its own definition, it pervades all of them equally.

28. Kelly Oliver, *Witnessing: Beyond Recognition* (Minneapolis, MN: University of Minnesota Press, 2001), 208.

29. Michael J. Sandel, *The Case against Perfection: Ethics in the Age of Genetic Engineering* (Cambridge, Mass: Belknap Press of Harvard University Press, 2007), 86.

30. Common sense suggests for some of us that the belief in immortality is a way of repressing the everyday reality of death. I do not necessarily disagree with this assessment. But my overall point is that we do this equally. Our diverse values are pervaded with infinite nonexistence, yet these values are never one with it. So even while we are equally exposed to our own groundlessness, nevertheless all of our values, even secular ones, posit some kind of myth that attempts to overcome this groundlessness. My argument is that we cannot measure which myths repress or assimilate this mortal groundlessness more than others since they all stand in relation to something infinitely elusive, something equally irreducible to all finite systems of belief.

31. Nevertheless, entropic affirmation is not equivalent to Foster's assessment of the death drive. It cannot be since he argues that being more open to the latter helps

us to fight back against systems of reification, whereas entropic affirmation rejects greater and lesser degrees of openness.

32. It may be worth repeating that entropic affirmation assumes that we are equally exposed to *and* removed from that which is infinitely irreducible. So in this way it is not a contradiction to claim, after having said that we are all equally open to unconditional loss, that we also turn away from and reject the meaninglessness of that loss. It is not a contradiction for the simple reason that what pervades all of our being nevertheless exceeds the contours of that same being, and thus it is impossible for us to fully embrace even that which we must necessarily embrace.

33. However, this doesn't imply that our values cannot be distinguished at all. There are many important differences between, for example, kindness and greed. The entropic argument only entails that such differences can never be made in relation to what is infinite.

34. None of this is to deny, in an empirical sense, that some of us are closer to death than others when, for example, we compare a healthy person to a terminally ill person. We can also compare standards of living in which there is no dispute that some of us live much safer and more comfortable lives than others. All that has been denied is that some cultural values are better attuned to the unknown than others, and this must be denied as there is no viable way of making that determination when the unknown infinitely exceeds and outstrips all such determinations.

35. Meaninglessness does not preclude meaning. If we have any values at all, then we ascribe meaning to the world and to our lives. But if this meaning ultimately breaks apart in an absolute sense, in the same way that death is the vanishing point of life, then it has a concrete relationship with its own nothingness and meaninglessness.

36. Luce Irigaray, *The Way of Love* (London; New York: Continuum, 2002), 172.

37. Irigaray, *To Be Two*, 73.

38. Ibid., 69.

39. Luce Irigaray, *An Ethics of Sexual Difference*, trans. Carolyn Burke (Ithaca, NY: Cornell University Press, 1993), 98; Luce Irigaray, *Éthique de la différence sexuelle* (Paris: Éditions de Minuit, 1984), 98.

40. Irigaray, *To Be Two*, 43.

Chapter 3

The Catastrophic Trajectory

In this chapter I argue that if change is both infinite and absolute then we cannot make predictive claims on the basis of whether or not we tend to reject its irreducible reality.[1] What I have in mind here is the sort of claim, found in a wide variety of authors to be discussed below, suggesting that the disavowal of something irreducible will lead to devastating consequences, along the lines of war and violence. But if there are no greater or lesser modes of disavowal in relation to irreducible otherness, as the previous chapter concluded, then such predictive claims are invalid. However, before elaborating this argument more fully, perhaps I should add that what is implied by change as something infinite is that it cannot be restricted by any limits or boundaries. There is no piece of reality that remains untouched by its transformative power. And when it is argued that it is absolute, what is meant is that such change brings about the disappearance of things (including life forms) without any hope of return. The disappearance is final, complete, and absolute.[2] So when change in this sense is being considered, it is true that what we have in mind is something irreducible to either a closed system or an eternal truth, for the simple reason that they themselves are open to its transformations.

There are, of course, other interpretations of change—and these will need to be considered below. In some cases it will be said that change is nothing more than illusion, while in others its reality is acknowledged albeit in such a way that denies absolute loss and death. If, however, it can be plausibly argued that change is limitless and death absolute, then there will be problems for any predictive trajectory stipulating that our rejection of irreducibility lends itself to catastrophic results, such as scapegoating, violence, and war.[3] The reason why problems arise—whether this irreducibility is associated with death, otherness, the uncanny, or any other language of the incommensurable—has to do with the impossibility of measuring what is immeasurable.[4]

27

So if it is true that death is a form of nothingness that cannot be reduced to the human constructs of moral evaluation, then we do not have the ability to say which values are less open to it than others—as it is the very definition of nothingness that it cannot be measured by means of an identifiable standard. And insofar as life and death are necessarily bound together, what is said about one can also be said about the other: there are no values or power relations that are less open than others to the inherent irreducibility of not only death but also life. So there are no degrees of difference, whether quantitatively or qualitatively speaking. And there will also be problems for those predictive trajectories, as we will see with Žižek and Butler, that conceptualize irreducibility more in terms of moral equality rather than infinite change or absolute death, except in these cases the problems will have more to do with an incorrect concept of what is irreducible rather than an incorrect inference that it can be measured.[5] Once these analyses have been concluded, it will be necessary to turn our attention to rethinking the relation between the meaning of our values (something that we cannot do without) and the infinity of change that exposes that meaning to its complete annihilation.

As noted, the catastrophic trajectory begins with something irreducible to closed systems. In this way it can be described as the real, the neighbor, the inhuman, nonidentity, singularity, precariousness, and so forth. This is not to suggest any kind of conflation here. What is meant by the real does not always include what is meant by nonidentity. So context is vital. Nevertheless, in the following discussion such terms will typically and broadly allude to a kind of reality that is irreducible to anything final, complete, closed, or self-identical. When Žižek distinguishes desire from *jouissance*, for instance, he does so in reference to an "undecipherable abyss."[6] It is by way of this abyss, Žižek argues, that desire is maintained. Without it, the desire for the other becomes suffocating; it becomes *jouissance*. So the difference in this context between the two is parallel to that between closure and that which resists closure, something irreducible to self-identity. And of course this difference can be stated in more than one way. Following Badiou and Rancière, Žižek teases out its political implications, for underlying every emancipatory movement is the demand that the excluded be identified with the whole of society. An oppressive politics aims at normalization, closure, and the subordination of the abyss within each of us to the smooth functioning of power. By contrast, an emancipatory politics emphasizes a kind of difference without a proper place in the whole, which is to say that it reverses the smooth functioning of the status quo: "This identification of the non-part with the Whole, of the part of society with no properly defined place within it (or resisting the allocated subordinated place within it) with the Universal, is the elementary gesture of politicization, discernible in all great democratic events."[7] So what cannot be contained by the whole comes to stand for it. And those who have no place in it become identified with it. A genuine universal approach to ethics and politics would therefore become more inclusive and more democratic without making essentialist assumptions about political identity. There is no humanist gesture here. There is no abstract universal category to which we all belong. Instead, for Žižek, what is universal and unites us is precisely that dimension within us that has no proper place or identity.

Depending upon the author, the inhuman dimension may or may not refer to something wholly and completely other. If we continue with Žižek for a moment, he states very clearly that he is primarily concerned with the real as an *effect* of the "gaps and inconsistencies" within symbolic space as opposed to the other way around.[8] There is nothing on the other side, or on the outside, of those gaps and inconsistencies that give rise to them. There is only the abyss or the real which is itself the symbolic eluding itself. In this sense we should do away with strict dichotomies between the symbolic and the real, as if the symbolic were a sort of obstacle or screen interfering with our direct access to something elusive beyond language, experience, and subjectivity. Adrian Johnston puts it quite well when he writes that the inaccessible, inhuman aspect of the real is nothing more and nothing less than subjectivity itself: "In other words, the horrible abyss of the Thing that Kant seeks to avoid is precisely this fantasmatic core of the subject's very being as subject, the hidden nucleus of its identity structure."[9] So what is unthinkable and unassimilable is not to be equated with something mystical, something existing beyond human perception and language. It is, rather, the symbolic itself which is its own limit and its own abyss. But it is also possible to think of our limits as being bound up with a mode of inaccessibility irreducible to the symbolic contours of language. In this case what is wholly other may refer to what Derrida describes as the secret. Although the secret pervades everything we think and say, and in this sense belongs to the symbolic, it would be a mistake to believe that it is thereby delimited or restricted. It is no contradiction, in other words, to suggest that what affects us may also transcend us. This is certainly what takes place, for example, when a river passes through and beyond each of its waves. In this sense the river should be described as both internal and external to those waves. Likewise, the wholly other that disrupts our ordinary patterns of thinking may do so from within those patterns even as it exceeds them. The implication would be that even as we are defined by our social conditions and experiences, there is always something remaining that cannot be accessed, something entirely secret and foreign. Derrida thus responds to critics who read him as a discursive constructivist that deconstruction always put into question the primacy and authority of language: "Deconstruction was inscribed in the 'linguistic turn,' when it was in fact a protest against linguistics!"[10] There should be no doubt, then, that Derrida and Žižek diverge from one another in terms of their metaphysics of what is secret, inhuman, or outside. But what they share, as alluded above, is the emphasis on irreducibility. In Derrida, no less than Žižek, it is the counterpoint to closure, control, and transparency that is crucial: "In consensus, in possible transparency, the secret is never broached. . . . If I am to share something, to communicate, objectify, thematize, the condition is that there be something non-thematizable, non-objectifiable, non-sharable. And this 'something' is an absolute secret."[11]

So whether or not the inhuman side of who we are is related to an extra-social or prelinguistic mode of alterity, in any case it suggests that we are not fully in control of our lives. It suggests that we are the sort of creatures who are marked by time, by the indetermination of the future. Every moment and every experience is therefore open to its own process of self-differentiation, a process that cannot be caged up or confined by any predetermined boundaries. Indeed, the fact that we attempt to exert control over our lives, through religion, politics, economics, technology, and so forth, lends itself to the insight that life is precarious. We are fragile beings who are easily wounded—by friends, by enemies, by natural disasters, by love, and by disease. And Judith Butler is right to argue that our exposure to loss implies that we are changed forever. On this basis, following well-known psychoanalytic categories, she distinguishes the work of mourning from the self-deception of melancholy: "Perhaps mourning has to do with agreeing to undergo a transformation (perhaps one should say *submitting* to a transformation) the full result of which one cannot know in advance."[12] Her parenthetical caveat is crucial. We ultimately submit to this process of change and transformation because we simply have no choice about it. If there were a choice involved, if our ultimate ontological condition were defined in terms of autonomy, then we would not be speaking of a genuine loss. In its place we would have in mind a temporary absence, as in the case of a friend who decides to take a short vacation. A genuine loss, however, is an irreversible loss. There is simply nothing that we can do to reverse the circumstances. And so according to the traditional distinction between mourning and melancholy, one may either accept this situation or resist it. But in neither case are we able to make ourselves whole and complete. Of course, in the familiar trajectory of ideas uniting the other, assimilation, and catastrophe, this temporal dimension of loss is regularly invoked. Bernard Stiegler writes that during times of major upheaval and rupture, it is paramount that we cultivate new processes of individuation and singularity. This involves affirming new ways of life that are irreducible to the modes of survival and commodification so prevalent today. And these new ways of life, as already alluded above, imply that we should remain open to the indetermination and uncertainty of the future. It is only on this basis, in other words, that we are able to avoid the melancholic façade of closure and completion: "The individual individuating itself is living . . . and when the individual reaches completion, this is because they have died. This incompletion is, as such, an irreducible trait of individu-*ation* insofar as it is a process, a process which, as the *becoming-other* of the one, is also a *becoming-multiple* of this one."[13] The process described here is without a doubt similar to that of mourning, in that the boundaries between the individual and the other, the one and the multiple, are affirmed as perpetually transient.

The denial of this process of becoming-other, if we continue this line of thought, is what leads to various forms of ideology. Stiegler thus argues that what we observe today under modern forms of cultural capitalism is the liquidation of singularity along with its openness to the future. And to the extent that it is a living subject who is involved in this liquidation, what we are observing is the reduction of our own lives to the *ethos* of mere subsistence—that is, instrumental survival: "This is true for everyone, consciously or otherwise, as a *global process of degradation*, where consciousness (conscious time) has become a commodity, the price of which is calculable in the marketplace."[14] Needless to say, ideology on this model doesn't operate in the traditional sense of propaganda whereby the content and the target of the message remain distinct in some identifiable way. The actualization of this model instead takes place through the very process of consumption and transformation. And what is lost is not only our unique singularity, as it is replaced by synchronized behavior patterns, but also our ability to feel the suffering of others. Žižek articulates this view explicitly when he writes that social atomism, contrary to the competing diagnoses of both the Right and the Left, works best when it is regulated by virtue of some neutralized background set of assumptions that unite us in our alienation.[15] So it is not exactly true that all social ties have been suspended under contemporary capitalism: we are bound together through an ideology that facilitates the smooth functioning of bio-politics, consumerism, and apathy. This explains the previous distinction made between two forms of universal ethics. In the first form what constitutes us as singular is denied, whereas in the second form it is acknowledged. For Žižek what is being rejected under the first version is the fact that we are not entirely human, that we will never be exactly identical with ourselves. There is no essentialist identity within us that lines up neatly with abstract notions of universality. To the contrary, to the extent that we are the mortal embodiments of desire, there is always something lurking within us that is monstrous and vulgar—an inhuman dimension. When this is disavowed we make it that much more difficult to identify with the suffering of others. In this sense every ethics that is established on the basis of an abstract universality, one which disavows the traumatic singularity of our existence, will draw some line between those who are properly human and those who are not. So if we want to avoid this ideological trap in which we inadvertently, or not so inadvertently, rationalize and perpetuate the suffering of others, we will need to rethink our concepts of universality: "The most difficult thing for common understanding is to grasp this speculative-dialectical reversal of the singularity of the subject *qua* Neighbor-Thing into universality, not standard 'general' universality, but universal singularity, the universality grounded in the subjective singularity extracted from all particular properties."[16]

Whereas Žižek contends that ideology requires the ongoing regulation of closure, as this process is never complete, others have been less restrained. Baudrillard and Virilio come to mind. In *Screened Out*, Baudrillard writes that the subject has already been liquidated, which is to say that the distance between ourselves and our virtual forms of existence has collapsed. In new forms of entertainment, social media, and consumption we are no longer able to separate what is real from the virtual interactions taking place on our screens. We have simply disappeared into the simulacrum of communication in which all opposites have become a single point of reference: "What was separated in the past is now everywhere merged; distance is abolished in all things: between the sexes, between opposite poles, between stage and auditorium, between the protagonists of action, between subject and object, between the real and its double."[17] The post-humanist logic here is not altogether different from what one observes in Žižek, as this virtual collapse of differences can be traced back to a technological and cultural systematization of all things incommensurable. For Baudrillard, however, it seems that we have now reached that critical stage in which the inhuman, alterity, and otherness have been finally vanquished: there is the simulacrum and nothing else. And Virilio's analysis provides us with the same theoretical assessment. He too understands the modern deployment of power and information as a kind of war against the real.[18] In this war on our senses everything that has depth is reduced to pure nothingness, such that we no longer have access to anything beyond our synchronized perceptions. The paradox is that we have lost contact with the void (or the abyss, the real, etc.) for the very reason that we have so fully integrated it into our networks of thought and perception: "If *escape velocity* effectively spells the world's old age, this is because the world itself must pass, be lost forever . . . having rammed two kinds of antagonistic desert end to end: the desert of *fullness* and the desert of the *vastness* of the cosmic void."[19] This suggests that the vastness of the void no longer exists for us. It no longer challenges us with its infinite mysteries and boundless depth. In its place there is only a flat, empty perception that reflects back to us our own digitalized expectations. And it is this empty, miserable condition which for several of these authors manifests pure ideology and pure control—regardless of more nuanced disagreements.[20]

All I have done thus far is outline the beginnings of a certain influential trajectory of thought. This trajectory begins with a disavowal of something that can be designated in numerous ways—as with the abyss or the inhuman.

However, it is not my suggestion that there is universal or widespread agreement on the details of this trajectory of thought. Disagreements are to be expected. But this shouldn't blind us to what many of these approaches share in common, especially when we consider a certain link between ideology and the immortal—or what is sometimes put forth in terms of bio-politics, transcendence, the metaphysics of presence, the desire for purity, totalized closure, and so forth. In each case we tend to disavow what is most intimate to us: our own fragile embodiment.[21] Perhaps the clearest statement of this view is to be found in Ernest Becker's *Escape from Evil* when he writes that all ideology "is about one's qualification for eternity."[22] It is through our cultural symbols that we humans entertain the possibility of escaping every kind of limit imaginable—including the one posed by death. We imagine that we are capable of rising above our own temporality in an effort to impose our will and our way of life on the universe, as if it must obey whatever we demand. This of course is far from the truth, which is why Becker describes this process in terms of cultural deception, mythmaking, and ideology. It is also why Žižek flips the switch by embracing what has been disavowed and excluded by such false promises. Having described the link between immortality and the good as a "traditional ideological commonplace," he thus writes that it is best to see this ruse for what it is—a mask for systematic control and violence.[23] As long as we subordinate all action to the demands of perpetual growth and development, to what can never be exposed to the alterity of weakness within each of us, we will find ourselves ideologically driven every step of the way. So we are hardly surprised when Žižek identifies the more radical good with the typically excluded element: "This is why the victory of good over evil is the ability to die, to regain the innocence of nature, to find peace in getting rid of the obscene infinity of evil."[24] It should also be added that what is disavowed is rarely identified with a self-contained experience. The embodied weakness inherent within all of us implies something profound about our relationships with others. For Butler, then, there is no vulnerability to loss without first of all assuming that the human body, along with our inevitable mortality, is socially constituted. It is because we are attached to others that we are at risk of losing what we love and care about. So the pervasive work of ideology is what manipulates and exploits this fear of loss by holding out the promise, directly or indirectly, of a world freed from the impurities of death, disease, and fragile relationships. And as alluded above, there is a culmination to this ideological trajectory, one which has devastating consequences.

The basic outline of this trajectory therefore begins with disavowal and typically ends with war, violence, and catastrophe. The disavowal, as already observed, is related to something that cannot be wished away—as with human mortality or the abyss of nothingness. And this explains for us what makes the disavowal ideological, as it attempts to accomplish the impossible by wishing away the very conditions of life that make desire and wishing conceivable.[25] It should be said once more, however, that the details of this trajectory are going to vary depending upon the author. In the case of Becker, for example, the underlying mechanism at work leading to violence and destruction is the antagonistic projection of inadequacy associated with scapegoating. When we take our group to be the ideal group, freed from the foulness of life identified with other groups—other races, cultures, and societies—at that point we are able to justify all sorts of heinous acts against those groups, as their very existence poses a threat to our cultural sense of superiority.[26] In addition to this process of scapegoating, Bataille highlights the forces of excess and expenditure within two different kinds of economy: restricted and general. In a restricted economy an attempt is made to subordinate excess energy to limited ends, although in truth this is impossible since that energy is infinite while our own ends are not. A general economy, by contrast, is not so reductionist. It is open to the fact that we are never fully in control of our lives, that everything we pursue succumbs to the extravagant expenditures of the universe that overturn and destroy all limited purposes and goals. As energy must be released in one way or another, Bataille's contention is that the restrictive economy is what leads to a catastrophic expenditure: "For if we do not have the force to destroy the surplus energy ourselves, it cannot be used, and, like an unbroken animal that cannot be trained, it is this energy that destroys us; it is we who pay the price of the inevitable explosion."[27] So in this variation what is emphasized is the economics of energy, but there are other versions of the trajectory in which energy plays no role at all. For Baudrillard what is most significant is the disappearance of our natural defenses. In the quest for perfection and immortality we replace natural selection (along with sex and death) with its artificial semblance, thereby increasing our chances of self-destruction: "For the death rate of artificial species is even more rapid than that of natural species. By taking an artificial course, our species may be running all the more quickly to its own decline."[28] It is clear, then, that there are several iterations of the catastrophic trajectory. Nevertheless, what I always have in mind as I continue to discuss these and other authors is the ideological disavowal of something irreducible (the inhuman, the neighbor, the unknown) that lends itself to highly destructive consequences.

As put forth above, the irreducible may or may not be wholly other. It may be something that not only traverses but also transcends our symbolic limits, but it may also be thought of as nothing more than how those limits are never exactly one with themselves. In both cases the irreducibility of the neighbor is something that we never fully grasp, yet the reasons given for this will diverge. And as the reasons diverge so too will the implications. If we look again at writers like Žižek and Butler, there's little doubt that they fall into the camp of elaborating this irreducibility in the direction of being fully socialized and symbolic—as opposed to being wholly or infinitely other. And when this sense of the neighbor is being considered what is often viewed as irreducible is the absolute moral equality embedded within all human beings. To reject this equality is thus to reject our intrinsic moral awareness. Restricting moral sympathy to only those who belong to *our* group, thereby arbitrarily establishing ourselves as culturally superior, is to reject the very principles of solidarity that we otherwise tend to embrace: "Refusing the same basic ethical rights to those outside our community as to those inside it is something that does not come naturally to a human being. It is a violation of our spontaneous ethical proclivity. It involves brutal repression and self-denial."[29] At this point it should be noted that Žižek's appeal to a "naïve ethical consciousness" is highly questionable. First of all, in terms of specific content, it's hardly a settled fact that human beings naturally resist "arbitrary" ethical distinctions between insiders and outsiders. In this respect, Lawrence Keeley's *War before Civilization* is a potent reminder that antagonistic group relations existed long before the advent of agriculture, urbanization, and state societies.[30] And in terms of form, apropos of the inner nature of our ethical proclivity, more than 2,000 years of philosophy, psychology, and social theory have failed to substantiate its existence *qua* "spontaneous." One therefore expects a detailed verification of this claim in Žižek's work, alongside his religious, political, historical, and other sophisticated analyses, but it is nowhere to be found. Nevertheless its influence can be felt everywhere in his overall development of thought. Divine violence is Žižek's ultimate political answer to the mounting injustices of modern civilization, and unsurprisingly it is defined as "pure drive."[31] It is unsurprising for the simple reason that it flows naturally from Žižek's formulation of the naïve moral disposition, as both the drive and the moral disposition are defined by their opposition to state power, instrumental reason, and the purity of justice: "The opposition of mythic and divine violence is that between the means and the sign, that is, mythic violence is a means to establish the rule of Law (the legal social order), while divine violence serves no means."[32] So there is a certain amount of logical consistency here, insofar as one form of purity leads to another; in the two cases of moral awareness and divine violence, the ideological dynamics associated with the Big Other are supposedly left behind.[33] But there is also a certain amount of inconsistency as soon as we compare Žižek's analysis of divine violence from the above quote with his interpretation of "ideology par excellence" elsewhere.[34] His definition of the latter as the rendering of background assumptions as nonideological is actualized as soon as divine violence is argued to be completely free from the influences of meaning, motive, and other objective criteria.[35] And once we are introduced to an interpretation of divine violence and divine justice as pure phenomena extracted from all ideological ends whatsoever, we should already know from Žižek himself that this is the first symptom of a radical ideology.

Butler's version of the argument also begins with an immediate apprehension of equality.[36] But what makes her version helpful here is that it explicitly formulates the logical progression from primary assumption to primary conclusion. While her analyses of how mainstream media frame issues of war, violence, and torture are both complex and insightful, the ethical argument underpinning these analyses is rather simple: *the apprehension of the shared precarious conditions of life implies that such life is marked by equal value.* So the initial phenomenological premise begins with an apprehension of the existential conditions of the other as precarious, fragile, and vulnerable. In turn, this apprehension implicates our own vulnerability, insofar as all living beings are at risk of death and destruction. Of course the ideological framing of the other attempts to deny this shared exposure to vulnerability, but the frames of war have their limits: "Another form of solicitation is also at work in such a frame, one that would lead us to an understanding of the equal value of life from an apprehension of shared precariousness."[37] So there is no doubt pertaining to the initial phenomenological assumption, and it is clear what is being derived from it in terms of ethics and politics, namely, that all life is equally valuable. But it remains unclear how the conclusion follows from the premise. While Butler states in a number of different places and contexts that the precarious conditions of life impose an ethical obligation on each of us, she never elaborates why this must be the case.[38] It's true that she avoids the fallacy of inferring social values from natural states of existence by defining our precarious conditions in terms of social dependency. In this way the existential or ontological basis of precariousness is coextensive with our need for others; we cannot have one without the other, and so there is no leap from fact to value in Butler's argument. The equal value of life is thus inferred from the social relations of interdependence that bind us together through ethical obligations: "These are not necessarily relations of love or even of care, but constitute obligations towards others, most of whom we cannot name and do not know, and who may or may not bear traits of familiarity to an established sense of who 'we' are."[39] But this clarification actually does more harm than good to Butler's egalitarian argument. If we want to say that all life is equally valuable, it doesn't help to base such value on the variable, changing relationships of mutual dependence. If these relationships prove anything, it is that we rely upon one another to varying degrees—and sometimes not at all.[40] Consequently, if there are varying degrees of dependence, belonging, and reliance, then the most obvious conclusion will lead us to the sorts of obligations that are equally diverse. So while it makes sense to observe that social and moral obligations arise from our everyday, concrete relationships, it is not clear what these obligations have to do with universal equality.

These critiques of Žižek and Butler have been immanent in nature, which is to say that they do nothing more than point out inconsistencies: (1) the pure drive associated with divine violence contradicts the notion that our actions can be entirely separated from instrumental ends; (2) there is nothing about the concept of vulnerability suggesting that all human life has equal value; and (3) such equality cannot be derived from its opposite, namely, *unequal* relations of dependence. Obviously, then, these are immanent critiques. But there is a larger methodological issue at stake here. For both of these writers the thing about us humans that can never be fully repressed, although it is often times attempted, is an underlying ethical form of equality. And if we were more attentive to this ethical starting point, we could do much more to fight back against war, injustice, and oppression. It could be argued, however, that the goal of social and political equality is manifested primarily on the level of representation as opposed to being that which can never be fully excluded.[41] If, that is to say, we wish to talk about an ethical starting point for that which necessarily resists every form of ideological homogenization, we will need to take seriously the idea that change is both infinite and absolute. It is infinite in the sense that it has no limits or boundaries, and it is absolute insofar as what is lost in the process of change is lost forever. Insofar as this can be shown to be the case, there will be consequences for the typical catastrophic trajectory. When this trajectory begins with a false assumption about our spontaneous moral condition, one that ascribes moral equivalence to the infinite movement of change that overturns all such equivalence, then the causal connections that are based on that trajectory are immediately called into question.[42] So the point being made here, to be as clear as possible, is that moral equality cannot be identified with the irreducible dimension of humanity if that equality is itself reducible to change and nothingness. A few remarks will therefore need to be said on behalf of this notion of change before proceeding any further.[43]

The easy argument would be to simply point out everyday observations in which entropic change appears to be the absolute condition of all things and all life. We are all familiar with the fact that people die, for example, and thus it appears to be that humans are mortal creatures who inevitably succumb to the pressures of space and time. But we are also familiar with theoretical and religious beliefs that deny such basic empirical observations. Some of these approaches to change challenge its very reality, thereby relegating it to an illusory realm of activity and perception, while others acknowledge its reality but deny the fact that it leads to a complete, irreversible loss. If we consider the first case for a moment, we'll notice that it tends to fall into two camps—the monistic and dualistic.[44] On the monistic side, the reality of change can be relegated to an illusory realm insofar as that change is nothing more than a manifestation of a single, unified reality. If, for example, we follow Chuang Tzu in repudiating the differences between *this* and *that*, the beginning and the end, or reality and dreaming, then we are left with the impression that all these things are ultimately the same.[45] And if this is right, then the experience of change and loss is reducible to the oneness of things that pervades all of the universe. But this is highly implausible. If all change is a manifestation of oneness, then it is impossible to explain the origins of its illusory nature. The experience of change cannot arise in a world which completely does away with all distinctions, as the experience itself is one more type of distinction. It can be retorted that such a distinction is still an illusion, and therefore doesn't truly exist, but this begs the question as to its reality *qua* illusion. For even if we grant that our experience of change, loss, and differentiation is somehow illusory, we still have no explanation for how this illusion *arises* in a world that never changes. By definition, a changeless world gives rise to absolutely nothing, and thus the experience of change, whether this experience is illusory or not, testifies to the fact that we do live in a changing world. So if there is any kind of illusion, it is specific in nature: it implies that I have confused one thing for another. But it does not prove that all things and objects are reducible to a single, all-pervasive reality. Quite the opposite: the illusion proves that I am *not* one with everything, that I am *not* a changeless entity, for the subject that is completely one with all things could never arise from that oneness as a separate entity capable of illusory experiences.

Another way of relegating change to a realm of illusion is by way of dualism. In this case, what is said to be temporal, changing, imperfect, and impure is associated with our physical embodiment. And, conversely, whatever is thought to be eternal, unchanging, perfect, and pure is associated with something deep within us—as with the soul, the mind, the forms of intellect, and so forth. Furthermore, if the two realms of purity and impurity can be kept separate from one another, then we don't have to engage the issue of origins raised above in reference to monism. If they are totally separate, in other words, then it would be incorrect to assume that one arises from the other in any problematic fashion—as all interaction is off the table. But if change is nothing more than pure illusion, and is thereby kept separate from the inner workings of the soul or the intellect, then we should ask ourselves how one realm becomes confused with the other. If I am fundamentally spirit, and the realm of physical embodiment is the realm of change and illusion, then what is spirit should not be susceptible of confusing itself with what is body. If my inner self is unchanging, then it cannot give rise to the illusion of being confused with what is external and thus changing. This contradiction is therefore not all that different from the one associated with monism. In both cases it becomes impossible to explain the origins of our experiences, many of which are associated with illusions, mistakes, physical embodiment, changing circumstances, and so forth. As we observed in monism, what is absolutely one with itself and all-pervasive cannot give rise to a subject that experiences itself as separate and changing. The same holds equally true from the other side of the equation: when the subject is said to be one with itself and unchanging, then it cannot in any way change into its opposite and experience itself as changing, temporal, and physical. Notwithstanding the brilliant efforts of Plato, Augustine, and Descartes, the attempt to reconcile eternity and change has always seemed forced. As soon as the "eternal" nature of the soul or the subject falls prey to the fluctuations of time and the inaccuracies of perception, it makes sense to reconsider the relationship between mind and body. The most plausible explanation for these tendencies, as modern psychology proves to us, is that the workings of the mind are plastic, embodied, and malleable.

It's also possible to think of change as a real phenomenon, albeit one that is reducible to a set of discrete elements. This view is no longer defended the way it once was in philosophy and physics, but its influence remains prevalent in the modern convergence of data-tracking, predictive analytics, artificial intelligence, work productivity, and targeted advertising. The intellectual traditions of Democritus and Hobbes live on when we hear about human consciousness being compared to computer networks—and thus reducible to bits of information that can be instantly tracked, analyzed, and commodified.[46] So the basic view of change being considered here—admittedly in broad terms—is one that truly affirms change but does so without affirming an irreversible loss.[47] There is no loss of substance or matter when change is equivalent to the organization and reorganization of data. On this model, change is nothing more than a shifting around of discrete elements which are themselves permanent. If that's correct, then it's possible—at least on a theoretical level—to reorganize the elements and thus bring back to life the previous formation of those same elements. Immortal life could therefore be achieved without positing an eternal soul that is distinct from the realm of change—as with the continual replacement of body parts with prosthetic devices. All that matters here is that change is the change of elements and parts, such that what has been "lost" can either be reinserted in its previous location or replaced by something equivalent. The problem with this assumption, however, is very similar to what we've already seen with the first two theories of change. In those theories what is illusory inevitably points to something real within the illusory. The experience of separation, for example, is not equivalent to pure illusion when the experience *itself* presumes some kind of break with the oneness of everything. Likewise in the case of discrete change: it is possible to think of our fluid experience of change in terms of something that is fixed and atomized, but the experience remains its own reality—something that is directly felt to be nonidentical.[48] In many ways the problematic assumption stems from the habits of language. When we speak of experience, we often times speak of an experience *of* something, as with the experience *of* change. This way of putting it makes it seem as if the change experienced is nothing more than an object of experience, understood to be outside of the experience itself, that is to say, entirely separate from it. But this is hardly the case.[49] To experience change is to experience a changing experience, an experience that is itself undergoing a transformation. So even if we hypothetically allow for the possibility that underlying this change is some kind of rearrangement of discrete elements, that would not preclude the fact that the experience itself is nonidentical, experienced on its own level as a phenomenon becoming something else, that is to say, becoming that which it is not—and therefore existing as that which it is *as well as* that which it is not. And as we have indicated above with the other theories of change, it doesn't help to argue that this experience is merely an illusion—for even if it is an illusion of some sort, the illusion is nonetheless its own reality, namely, the kind of reality that is nonidentical to itself and experienced as such.

At the very least, then, fluid change is real—even if this means that its reality is restricted to the surface level of human phenomenology. And if it *is* so restricted, then the experience of absolute loss isn't necessarily final, because it will always remain possible, at least theoretically, to rearrange the underlying elements of change into their previous formation prior to the loss. But in showing that there is something real about the experience of nonidentity, which is the experience of fluid change,[50] it can be extrapolated that it is precisely this kind of change that resists being confined to permanent boundaries. As soon as we try to create those boundaries between discrete and indiscrete change, we fail miserably. By definition, it is the latter kind of change that is nonidentical and therefore overflows itself. This implies that all of its interactions are defined by this overflowing, which is another way of saying that the "elements" of space and time that support, frame, or embody these fluid interactions cannot themselves remain discrete. Nor does it help to argue that the experience of this nonidentical change is *only* an experience, because the experience is nonetheless something happening and embodied. And to the extent that the experience is embodied in such a way that it is finite, temporal, and overflowing—which is to say indiscrete—then the embodiment is not some kind of external container that remains separate or unaffected by the experience of overflowing change. This may look and sound like an abstract argument, but it is supported by the everyday observation that the kind of body which gives rise to experience is a body in which all of its parts—whether physiological, genetic, psychological, or social—are perpetually affected by a multitude of outside forces. This same overall perspective that change overturns all boundaries can also be found in the likes of Rosi Braidotti, who draws inspiration from Spinoza and Deleuze in arguing that nothing escapes the self-differentiating processes of radical immanence.[51] What this means is that the processes of change take place without regard to sharply defined limits or dichotomies. All such dichotomies are themselves subject to change, and thus they cannot support the fiction of any kind of reality that remains precisely what it is from one moment to the next. This notion of fluid, overflowing change is best described as infinite for the simple reason that it defies and deconstructs all permanent limits. But whether or not the infinite nature of change implies that what changes involves an absolute loss, or an absolute death, is an open, debatable issue. Braidotti herself is opposed to this view on the grounds that it leads to a pessimistic vision of politics and power.[52] It is therefore possible to consider two broad concepts of infinite otherness and change: one that rejects absolute loss and another that embraces it.

In the first concept every mode of loss, including that of death, is taken to be a subordinate phase within a larger process of *zoe*, growth, and cosmic energy. So it is true for Braidotti that we never escape this overflowing process of change and becoming, yet this does not imply that death is either final or absolute for us: "Death is the ultimate transposition, though it is not final, as *zoe* carries on, relentlessly. Death is the inhuman conceptual excess. . . . Yet death is also a creative synthesis of flows, energies and perpetual becoming."[53] This is an affirmative, positive view of death, one which sees death as the triumph of life over isolated moments of individuality. So what happens when we die is that we merge with the forces of life that surround, pervade, and overwhelm us, and there should be nothing pessimistic about this. The entire process of death is one of life-affirmation, and it is only our shortsighted attachment to the self or ego that makes us think otherwise. But if this is right, how do we explain the origins of our shortsighted, negative emotions? They are often times based on immaturity or misinformation, as when I react defensively in the face of a well-intentioned criticism. But in the general, existential sense of death, if it is in every respect composed of positive, life-affirming forces, how is it that we come to perceive these forces as their very opposite? The illusion, as intimated above, may arise from the fact that we are unduly attached to the finitude of the ego. But this response only goes so far. If every single moment of change is generative and life-affirming, then there is nothing in that experience of change that could be perceived as loss. The whole process of life, including that of undergoing change and dying, could only ever be felt as one of constant growth, development, and progress. All the instincts and desires of the self would become strengthened and fortified as they developed closer ties with the other forces and energies of life all around us. Nothing would ever be felt or experienced as a movement of loss, as nothing within us—including all of our emotions and desires—would in any respect undergo such a loss. Nor does it help to say that the problem arises on the level of shortsightedness, in the sense that we're unable to foresee the good consequences of all of these changes, since all we would ever experience in the moment, in the here and now, would be the same exhilaration of life that should also be expected in the future. In sum, if all change is generative, then so too is the experience of that change; there is no experience of pain or loss if all such experience overflows with positivity. As with the earlier "illusions" of separation, embodiment, and overflowing change, the ones pertaining to our negative emotions (e.g., fear, anxiety, and anger) likewise gesture toward something real—in this case the reality of absolute loss. The inference to be drawn, then, is that change *qua* infinite and *qua* absolute is real. It will never be stopped or contained by the human constructs of eternal truth, discrete elements, or the immortal soul. And although some of our anxieties are truly misguided and misinformed, the fact that we are the sorts of creatures prone to such emotions ought to remind us that we are indeed familiar with the kind of change that does away with the substance of our lives in a permanent, irreversible fashion.

This conclusion should make us question the catastrophic trajectory. In the cases in which it posits an irreducible element distinguished from change that is both infinite and absolute, the trajectory begins with an incorrect assumption. It is true, as Butler puts forth, that all life is equally precarious. But it is so for the very reason that life is bound up with the absolute nature of death. We are all vulnerable and weak in this sense, and thus it cannot be plausibly argued that we have access to values that transcend this point of reference. Butler and Žižek, however, would like to infer from our existential precariousness a certain kind of social value that is both consistent with this precariousness as well as irreducible to it. The social value of equality is therefore said to be the irreducible element from which we should never deviate, as doing so increases the likelihood of a catastrophic trajectory—one that involves scapegoating, violence, war, environmental destruction, and so forth. Needless to say, there are many courses of action that do in fact bring about such results, but the analysis of such tendencies has nothing to do with values (as with the equality of life) that are irreducible to anything else—values that are said to be inherent to our very nature. It cannot have anything to do with them as they simply do not exist. Insofar as change is infinite and absolute, whatever values that we create are themselves permeated by this ontological condition—and so in all cases are reducible to it.[54] If it were the other way around, if these values were completely generative, then the meaninglessness of death would be relative, conditional, and temporary, but as we have shown above (in response to Braidotti) this is hardly the case. As a consequence, any theory of values that posits those values as irreducible to the infinity of change—values that are purely social, generative, spiritual, dialectical, teleological, and so forth—is a theory that begins with a false premise. In this regard every version of the catastrophic trajectory that relies upon such values needs to be rejected.

But we mustn't forget the alternative interpretations of this trajectory. Some versions of it, as we have seen, begin with the premise that the other is wholly and entirely other. What is meant here in a precise sense will depend upon the author in question, but as far as the overall catastrophic trajectory is concerned the specifics are irrelevant. What matters for writers like Bataille, Becker, Kristeva, and Derrida is that something be acknowledged as irreducible to the positivity of presence. This is what J. Hillis Miller has in mind when he discusses the deconstructive role of the *tout autre* in Derrida's ethics: "The notion of a justice that is wholly other explains why Derrida . . . develops further the idea that the moment of decision is not present."[55] The ethical decision can never be fully present to itself, never fully under rational control, because it responds to the limitless, infinite call of responsibility associated with the *tout autre*. And although Miller concedes that the principle of self-destruction is at work in every community to some extent, he makes the familiar argument that this process is magnified under the right conditions—as when we overreach our natural and social limitations in an attempt to subordinate what is infinitely other to various anthropomorphic ideals, whether by religion, technology, politics, etc.[56] This argument, however, contradicts entropic affirmation—that is, the principle that all values and practices affirm what is limitless to the same degree. If change is truly infinite and absolute, then there is no value that can be said to be more closely aligned with it than any other. If there is indeed something meaningless about death, something that cannot be recuperated by human values—which is not to say that we experience change and death apart from such values—then whatever meaning we assign to it will be just as mythological as any other.[57] It may be easy for some to observe how the value and meaning of God represents an impossible attempt to overcome the finality of death, and so the attempt is described as misguided, irrational, and mythological. But it's not as if we have access to a different set of values that are any more enlightened.[58] At first it seems possible to be less anthropocentric (and thus more open) in the face of death's nothingness, but if this nothingness is truly infinite, then it is impossible to measure any differences in relationship to it—whether quantitatively or qualitatively speaking. Hence the position that some values and practices give rise to destructive consequences whenever they assimilate or exclude what can never be fully assimilated or excluded—as it is an irreducible element of some kind—is highly questionable. In the first place, it has never been empirically tested or verified. Secondly, if what is irreducible is said to be something other than infinite change, then the argument begins with a false premise. And lastly, if it does begin with the more plausible premise that what is other is infinitely other, as we see with Miller, then we cannot infer any predictive trajectory from such a premise, as the reality of limitlessness transcends all values and practices equally.

This critique does not deny the reality of various destructive tendencies. But when violence, war, and catastrophe are explained in terms of how certain power dynamics, whether by means of exclusion or assimilation, relate to the irreducible elements of our existence, it is impossible to verify such claims. It might therefore be inferred that the best thing to do is take up a more pragmatic approach, one that moves beyond the terminology of infinite otherness and irreducible phenomena. In this vein, Habermas responds to Bataille's distinction between unproductive expenditures and catastrophic tendencies by explicitly rejecting the role of incommensurability in rational theory:

> If the other of reason is more than just the irrational or the unknown—namely, the *incommensurable*, which cannot be touched by reason except at the cost of an explosion of the rational subject—then there is no possibility of a theory that reaches beyond the horizon of what is accessible to reason and thematizes, let alone analyzes, the interaction of reason with a transcendent source of power.[59]

The false assumption here is that reason has no access to what is wholly and infinitely other. By definition, if the otherness of change is infinite, then it necessarily pervades all aspects of our existence, including rational communication and theory. So from the fact that we are unable to distinguish between greater and lesser forms of openness vis-à-vis the incommensurability of change, it should not be inferred that such incommensurability plays no role at all in the determination of our values. It's possible, in other words, to critique Bataille's thinking of catastrophe without thereby reinterpreting all forms of otherness as fundamentally social, pragmatic, diacritical, etc. And if the critique doesn't fall back on these types of reinterpretations, then it will necessitate a new methodology—one that emphasizes the radical nature of heterogeneity in the formation of our values without claiming that these values need to be more open to this heterogeneity in order to avoid catastrophe. These values will certainly have social and pragmatic dimensions, but insofar as the heterogeneity of change will always pervade them, they will always affirm their own demise—which implies that their social and pragmatic dimensions will be limited. But if it is true that all values affirm the nothingness of death equally, then an explanation is required as to what role it plays in the construction of those same values. If this role cannot be explained, then our so-called new methodology hasn't provided us with any new insights about the nature of ethics. It will therefore be the task of the next chapter to make some progress in this direction.

NOTES

1. In the following argument I will not assume that predictive trajectories must follow a strict causal chain from the disavowal of change to catastrophic results. It will thus be argued that there is no connection whatsoever, strong or weak, between the rejection of something irreducible and catastrophic tendencies.

2. These terms will be elaborated in more detail in the following pages.

3. Although I will sometimes use the negative language of rejection, repression, and disavowal, it should be understood that such denials can be taken in a very broad sense. For example, it can be argued that power today works by way of positive assimilation, as Foucault, Butler, Agamben, and others have clearly shown. In this way it's quite possible that the assimilation and disavowal of otherness work together simultaneously.

4. I began this chapter by associating change and death with infinity, but I would like to be flexible enough to include other philosophical terminology—as with alterity, singularity, the uncanny, and so on. I think this flexibility is justified due to the way in which change affects all things, so that it only makes sense to extend its influence to the way in which life is always singular, uncanny, incommensurable, and so forth.

5. Of course, some of those whom I critique in this way, such as Derrida and Bataille, would agree that what is infinite (as with infinite responsibility) cannot be measured. But I will argue that they nonetheless assume the contrary whenever they posit that some forms of power or values are more open than others to what is absolutely other.

6. Slavoj Žižek, *The Puppet and the Dwarf: The Perverse Core of Christianity* (Cambridge, Mass: MIT Press, 2003), 61.

7. Ibid., 65.

8. Ibid., 66.

9. Adrian Johnston, *Žižek's Ontology: A Transcendental Materialist Theory of Subjectivity* (Evanston, Ill: Northwestern University Press, 2008), 33.

10. Jacques Derrida et al., *A Taste for the Secret*, trans. Giacomo Donis (Malden, MA: Polity, 2001), 76.

11. Ibid., 57.

12. Judith Butler, *Precarious Life: The Powers of Mourning and Violence* (London and New York: Verso, 2006), 21.

13. Bernard Stiegler, *Decadence of Industrial Democracies*, trans. Daniel Ross, vol. I (Cambridge: Polity, 2011), 38.

14. Ibid., 29.

15. Slavoj Žižek, *In Defense of Lost Causes* (London and New York: Verso, 2008), 34.

16. Ibid., 16–17.

17. Jean Baudrillard, *Screened Out*, trans. Chris Turner (London and New York: Verso, 2002), 176.

18. Paul Virilio, *City of Panic*, trans. Julie Rose (Oxford and New York: Berg, 2005), 34.

19. Ibid., 114.

20. See for example Baudrillard's critique of Virilio's "final accident." Baudrillard, 110.

21. This concrete embodiment is not impervious to the fluctuations of change and otherness. So what is most intimate is precisely that which is open to the outside. It is not a private affair. The embodiment being discussed, then, is neither self-sufficient nor self-enclosed. Indeed, it would be very odd if the quest for immortality and perfection were *not* disavowing that kind of embodiment which remains open to the real uncertainties of life.

22. Becker, *Escape from Evil*, 116.

23. Slavoj Žižek, *Violence: Six Sideways Reflections* (New York: Picador, 2008), 65.

24. Ibid., 66.

25. Put another way, ideological desire is attempting to do away with itself by overcoming its inherent lack and finitude. But as I will try to show below, this is impossible as long as we acknowledge the reality and pervasiveness of change—for as long as there is change all of our accomplishments are finite, fragile, and temporary.

26. Becker, *Escape from Evil*, 93.

27. Georges Bataille, *The Accursed Share: An Essay on General Economy: Consumption*, trans. Robert Hurley (New York: Zone Books, 1988), 24; Georges Bataille, *La part maudite: précédé de la notion de dépense* (Paris: Éditions de Minuit, 1967), 62.

28. Jean Baudrillard, *The Vital Illusion* (New York: Columbia University Press, 2000), 18.

29. Žižek, *Violence: Six Sideways Reflections*, 48.

30. Lawrence H Keeley, *War before Civilization* (Oxford: Oxford University Press, 1996).

31. Žižek, *Violence: Six Sideways Reflections*, 198.

32. Ibid., 199.

33. Ibid., 200.

34. Žižek, *In Defense of Lost Causes*, 21.

35. Objective criteria are understood here to imply any sort of externally identifiable qualities that would distinguish divine from mythic violence. But this is what Žižek explicitly rejects in the context of the above quoted passages.

36. The two versions of ethical apprehension diverge in terms of their theoretical influences—Lacanian in one case and Levinasian in the other—but that does not preclude them from sharing a common trajectory by way of which the denial of our immediate apprehension of equality lends itself to war and violence.

37. Judith Butler, *Frames of War: When Is Life Grievable?*, Pbk. ed. (London and New York: Verso, 2010), xvi.

38. Unless we count the kind of assertion that is found in the quote below. But it should be fairly clear that the equality of rights or values cannot be derived from their antithesis—that is, relationships in which we rely upon one another to varying degrees.

39. Butler, *Frames of War: When Is Life Grievable?*, xxvi.

40. In a certain sense, it is obvious that Butler acknowledges this. Why else does she critique differential allocations of violence and suffering unless she recognizes the variable networks of interaction that give rise to those same allocations? But this critique is inconsistent as it derives a universal principle of equality from an unevenly actualized reality of mutual dependence in order to then critique that reality for its lack of universal application.

41. Representation is here being associated with socially constructed ideals, in contrast with a notion of change that permeates all things without being reduced to them.

42. Perhaps it should be noted here that the meaninglessness associated with absolute loss does not preclude all forms of morality. There is a certain nihilism associated with thanato-vitalism insofar as this method affirms the utter destruction of embodied values in the face of emptiness and death. The method also critiques moral systems that attempt to translate that emptiness into fullness, as when it said that precariousness is ultimately a social phenomenon. But the emptiness of death does not preclude the reality of social values. To the contrary, it simply exposes their limit. The challenge, then, is to articulate a view of ethics that acknowledges this limit without thereby losing sight of the significant role of moral values in all of our lives.

43. These remarks proceed indirectly in that they eliminate other theories of change in hopes of making my own view more plausible. The first two theories relegate change to the realm of illusion, while the last two accept its reality without thereby accepting absolute loss (i.e., the vanishing of things into nothingness). By process of elimination, then, if these theories fall short of explaining our basic, everyday experiences of change and loss, then it should strike us as all the more reasonable to affirm change as a real process involving real loss.

44. This is not say that all monists or dualists can be categorized in this way. As we'll see shortly, for example, Rosi Braidotti is a monist who embraces the reality of change while rejecting the prioritization of loss and death.

45. Chuang Tzu, *Chuang Tzu: Basic Writings*, trans. Burton Watson (New York: Columbia University Press, 1996).

46. Chapter 8 from Ray Kurzweil's *How to Create a Mind* is a notable exemplification of this tendency. Ray Kurzweil, *How to Create a Mind: The Secret of Human Thought Revealed* (New York: Viking, 2012).

47. I am considering these different views of change in broad terms because the problems that arise for each one are themselves general in nature. So, for example, if eternity and change are irreconcilable on any level, then it doesn't matter whether we have in mind Plato's forms or Augustine's creator of the universe. Likewise here, as I will argue: change is irreducible to discrete elements, and it simply doesn't matter if those elements are expressed in terms of atoms or bits of data.

48. If the experience were self-identical it would be one with itself, which is another way of saying that it would be fully transparent to itself without any hidden mysteries. But since every time we attempt to freeze a moment of time or experience so that it is completely transparent to itself we always fail, it is more plausible to describe such a moment as nonidentical (as I will continue to do).

49. This is not to claim that objects are reducible to changing subjects. They are not completely identical, as that would contradict earlier statements rejecting monistic

oneness. Instead, what I perceive to be changing is part of my experience and thus affects me—so that the experience of change is necessarily the experience of a changing experience, without this implying any collapse of differences into oneness.

50. Discrete elements are identical to themselves insofar as they are never permeated by that which exists outside of themselves (i.e., permeated by otherness and change). By contrast, then, indiscrete change proceeds by way of that which is non-identical, by the flow of change that perpetually overturns limits and boundaries.

51. Braidotti, *The Posthuman,* 56.

52. Ibid., 121.

53. Ibid., 131.

54. For purposes of terminological clarity, change is infinite in the sense that it has no bounds or limits, but it is also absolute insofar as it is connected to the disappearance of things—a phenomenon that can never be overcome or vanquished. Although the term "absolute" may be better reserved for such a disappearance of things (as with the death of a friend), the fact that change cannot be understood apart from how things disappear in an absolute way suggests that it can be described not only as infinite but also as absolute.

55. J. Hillis Miller, *For Derrida* (New York: Fordham University Press, 2009), 19.

56. Ibid., 123–26.

57. One objection might be that if death ultimately transcends all of our values and meanings then we should stop projecting them onto it. In that way we wouldn't fall prey to the fallacies associated with our anthropomorphic ideals. But this objection doesn't hold. Entropic affirmation holds not only that all values affirm the absoluteness of death equally, but that furthermore they necessarily affirm it. We cannot avoid affirming change and death if they permeate every moment of life. In other words, insofar as there is an infinite aspect to change, every value affirms some part of reality which is itself a manifestation of that infinite flux. All values therefore affirm death in some fashion or another, and do so tragically and mythologically.

58. That's not to say that all values are the same, but only that their differences cannot be based on how open they are to the fundamental alterity, otherness, and change that permeates all things.

59. Jürgen Habermas, *The Philosophical Discourse of Modernity: Twelve Lectures,* trans. Frederick G. Lawrence (Cambridge, Mass: MIT Press, 1987), 235–36.

Chapter 4

Expansive Singularities

It's possible to imagine the will to power and the will to nothingness as different kinds of willing, as if they were entirely separate from one another.[1] In the first case the will to power represents an approach to life which seeks to enhance itself by overcoming obstacles and points of resistance. In the second case it gives up on itself by seeking refuge in the nothingness of a life beyond life—an ideal form of life that exists without any source of struggle, friction, or conflict. If we take this distinction at face value, then Leonard Lawlor is right that "Heidegger's conception of Nietzsche's idea that life is will to power, and Foucault's conception of the modern regime of power as bio-power are similar if not identical conceptions."[2] But the opposite may also hold true. If the will to nothingness, for Nietzsche, is to be associated with a weak type of person, with someone who avoids the realities of death and finitude, then the formations of bio-power that seek *only* to preserve and enhance life should be aligned with the will to nothingness rather than the will to power. The inference would be that the will to power, contrary to Heidegger's conception, would not only be defined by its attempt to preserve and enhance itself, but also by its courage in the face of its own demise. In this way it could be argued, despite the misleading language, that it is the will to power rather than the will to nothingness which is more open to actual nothingness—as with the actual nothingness of death.[3] This distinction, however, should also be questioned. What does it mean to say that one set of values is more open than another to the emptiness and nothingness of death? If this absence of life has no inherent meaning or value, then it would seem to follow that all of our categories of analysis would hold the same incommensurable relationship to it.[4] But if we can't distinguish our values and categories in this way, as if some were more open to nothingness than others, then what role does death play in the construction of those values? Does it amount to nothing at all?

I do not think so. Instead I will argue that the emptiness of death predisposes all of our values to be affirmed as expansive singularities, which is to say that their enhancement and destruction will always be affirmed together. And if this proves to be correct, then it will follow that any critique of values based on their tendency to seek nothing more than what is positive—as with their own security, proliferation, and enhancement—will be deeply misguided.[5]

I would like to begin with a series of quotes and references that will highlight an influential line of thought in contemporary cultural studies. This line of thought focuses on the malign pervasiveness of instrumental rationality. Hence, as with Butler's *Frames of War*, it may be argued that when we perceive others as the instruments of our own power we are more likely to see them as being "framed by the tactics of war."[6] In a similar vein, Stiegler warns that when human inventiveness collapses into nothing more than an "*adaptive* process of *survival*" or "simple modalities of subsistence" we end up with violent social and political models: "It is for this reason that the United States has been led into war, however much the accidental motives for this war may be tied to the apparently unbalanced psychological personalities of those such as George Bush and Osama bin Laden."[7] Irigaray adds that in today's age of technique we forget how to grow, blossom, and cultivate ourselves: "The blossoming of man requires, in fact, a making and a letting be."[8] The implication is that we have become very good at making, which is a manifestation of control and objectification, while at the same time we are losing the art of acceptance. Much of the problem has to do with our excess reliance on technological developments. Whatever it is within us that makes us interesting, mysterious, or unique is being sacrificed in the name of satisfying as many of our interests as possible in the most convenient way possible. Agamben thus writes that "today there is not even a single instant in which the life of individuals is not modeled, contaminated, or controlled by some apparatus."[9] It should be said here that Agamben's reference to the apparatus (or *dispositif*), borrowed from Foucault, is broadly construed to apply to any social development that shapes human existence. So these processes have existed for a very long time, since at least the advent of language, but what makes them dangerous today is their unprecedented proliferation. Stefan Herbrechter sees the peril in this as one in which we ourselves become mere automata: "This ideology of development and (self)-transformation has become automated . . . and is now threatening to become the embodiment of the inhuman or even the posthuman, because, for the complex system, humans are merely a means to an end."[10] And as we assimilate ourselves to the practices of instrumental power, we eventually replace the will to power with the will to nothingness. We do this because we no longer seek out problems and obstacles to overcome, but prefer instead to alleviate as much pain and suffering as possible. Baudrillard spoke of this in terms of transferring the burdens of life and intelligence to machines that would do the thinking for us: "If men dream of machines that are unique, that are endowed with genius, it is because they despair of their own uniqueness, or because they prefer to do without."[11] What Baudrillard doesn't say explicitly in this particular quote can nonetheless be surmised from the vast majority of his writing, namely, that we ourselves our becoming the machines that do nothing but calculate results.

Paul Rabinow and Nikolas Rose are right to resist interpretations of bio-power that reduce all of its manifestations to a "single configuration" or "unified strategy," especially one that posits murder and killing as its primary objective.[12] This they do in response to certain all-too-general claims that have been made by Agamben, Hardt, and Negri. Nevertheless, modern regimes of power in Foucault's work are typically analyzed in the context of their calculative investments in life—investments that ultimately lend themselves to the killing of others, whether directly or indirectly, by means of state racism. Foucault goes so far as to say that for this reason "the modern state can scarcely function without becoming involved with racism at some point," which implies that the power of making live is ultimately broken up and fragmented in order to justify the death of others.[13] Hence the most significant problem with power today, structurally speaking, has less to do with one of its particular manifestations, as with an inappropriate goal or objective, than with its overall strategic orientation.[14] So it is the obsession with calculation itself vis-à-vis life-enhancement that needs to be rethought if we wish to avoid the devastating consequences of perpetual conflict. This can be discerned from numerous passages in a variety of texts.[15] In the *History of Sexuality*, volume 1, Foucault writes that modern power relations are "imbued, through and through, with calculation."[16] Now, if the main problem with these relations had to do with their *particular* strategies and calculations, as opposed to instrumental rationality in general, it is doubtful that Foucault, in the same volume, would provide us with an alternative way of thinking about the relationship between pleasure and power—one that seemingly avoids the catastrophic consequences of the more instrumental approach.[17] In one of the most highly critiqued (and perhaps misunderstood) passages, Foucault argues that "bodies and pleasures" should form the basis for a counterattack against modern power regimes, as with the deployment of sexuality that has become nearly ubiquitous. The critique made by Butler, Grosz, Agamben, and many others is that Foucault seems to have forgotten that there is no such thing as bodies and pleasures existing outside of their historical circumstances.[18] In other words, he has forgotten, that is to say, the trajectory of analytics that he himself forged in painstaking detail for several years prior to penning those unfortunate last lines of the *History of Sexuality*, volume 1. But this is an uncharitable reading of Foucault. In an earlier part of the book, under *Scientia Sexualis*, he observes that in other traditions pleasure isn't considered in "reference to a criterion of utility, but first and foremost in relation to itself."[19] This understanding of pleasure (from ancient Rome to India and China) doesn't do away with truth and power, but provides us with a different relationship. Instead of subordinating bodies and pleasures to instrumental aims that invest and control those pleasures with rational tendencies, it is the reality of those bodies and pleasures without inherent aims that must first be addressed. So there is no reification of reality outside of all social tendencies, as if Foucault were putting his own methodology on hold, but simply a reconsideration of life beyond the controls of administered calculations.

As intimated above, I do not think that the distinction between a will to power (one which affirms death and finitude) and a will to nothingness (thus far considered as instrumental life-enhancement) is viable. I do not even think that the distinction is viable in terms of degrees, in the sense that some forms of power are relatively, if not absolutely, more open than others to the inherent aimlessness of life.[20] The power structures that define us can only be said to be more or less open to *particular* forms of life, death, and finitude—not to any of them in a *general* sense.[21] But this isn't Foucault's approach. Already we've seen from his argument in the first volume of the *History of Sexuality* (and the last lecture of *Society Must Be Defended*) that it is our obsession with life itself, maximizing as many of its tendencies and attributes as possible, that gives rise to the problematic paradoxes of modern violence and racism. If it were only a particular form of life-maximization that were so problematic, then Foucault would be less likely to make references to "life in general" or "life in itself" as he so often does. Hence, when elaborating the role of bodies and populations in the development of capitalism, what was needed was "to have methods of power capable of optimizing forces, aptitudes, and life in general."[22] Similarly, these methods no longer focused on threats of death or torture, but increasingly relied upon techniques of application "at the level of life itself."[23] And in this way Foucault surmises that today's mode of power has "taken control of both the body and life or that has, if you like, taken control of life in general."[24] Keeping in mind that Foucault is a non-essentialist, phrases like "life in general" and "life in itself" are somewhat enigmatic. But if we are contrasting a modern form of power that is defined by its calculative operations with something that doesn't entirely fit with those operations—for if the overall movement of life were immune to all threats and dangers then there would be no sense of reinforcing it with such life-enhancing powers—it would seem to follow that what is meant by "life in itself" would have something to do with its inherent fragility, with the way in which it is ineluctably bound up with death, weakness, and uselessness. It thus follows, insofar as Foucault describes power as being entirely imbued with calculation, that the primary function of such power is to transform as much of life as possible into that which it is not: *a functional and strategic set of operations with no weakness whatsoever.*

So the modus operandi of both discipline and bio-power is that of strategic utility. Everything that defines us—from desires and pleasures to aptitudes and thoughts—will always have this function. On the individualized scale of discipline, every moment of time is a potential resource to be mined for maximum efficiency: "Discipline . . . arranges a positive economy; it poses the principle of a theoretically ever-growing use of time, ever more available moments and, from each moment, ever more useful forces."[25] We must therefore take advantage of every opportunity to build up these forces to make ourselves healthier, stronger, and more efficient, as the failure to do so exposes us to unnecessary risks. And it is this pressure to avoid weakness at all costs that inevitably transforms us into machines. Foucault thus speaks of the modern soldier of the late eighteenth century as someone who is mastered, pliable, and automatized: "The soldier has become something that can be made; out of a formless clay, an inapt body, the machine required can be constructed."[26] It's not difficult to see why Foucault makes such a comparison: the more we subordinate ourselves to calculated results, the more we see ourselves as the predetermined means for achieving those results. Although it is important to keep in mind that the typical dichotomies between the means and ends of power are blurred when the body itself has become a target of that power. So when Foucault speaks of increased aptitudes as the instantiation of increased domination, it is evident that the creation of the modern soldier is itself one of the primary aims of discipline.[27] This is equally true even in those cases in which power allows for a certain degree of freedom in the formation of modern economic subjects. So in the early sections of *The Birth of Biopolitics*, Foucault refers to the self-imposed limits of governmental reason as something that must be derived from interest.[28] This implies that those same limits go hand in hand with a proliferation of subjects who are manageable precisely because their conduct is rational, calculative, strategic, self-interested, and machine-like.[29] And as the partner of exchange ultimately gives way to a version of *homo œconomicus* in which the subject becomes human capital, it is fair to say that the laissez-faire attitude of governmental reason becomes all the more conducive to the spread of instrumental calculations. As long as we think of ourselves in terms of capital, as being entrepreneurs of ourselves, it becomes all the more imperative to think of our minds and bodies as the objects of perpetual investments. Hence Foucault's characterization of a mother's attention to her child as one factor among many that contributes to the formation of an "abilities-machine."[30] The so-called privacy of the home, then, is nothing of the sort. We may have rights to privacy under a neoliberal version of democracy, but these rights that guarantee a certain amount of freedom are essential to the coercion of subjects who can be relied upon to respond to manipulated social environments (through media, technology, education, etc.) in a nonrandom, useful, life-enhancing way. If power has become increasingly focused on strategic rationality, then the transition from the sovereign point of view to neoliberal economics is a transition which involves the intimate connection between atomistic freedom and self-governance: "*Homo œconomicus* is the one island of rationality possible within an economic process whose uncontrollable nature does not challenge, but instead founds the rationality of the atomistic behavior of *homo œconomicus*."[31]

As I will argue below, it does not seem correct that we can affirm the maximization of life forces apart from their eventual demise. To affirm life is also to affirm death. But it does seem at first glance that what Foucault and others have described as the modern compulsion of power is nothing less than a desire to do away with death. It may be that we no longer rely so heavily on the mechanisms of either repression or negativity, but there is still an attempt to separate life as much as possible from death. In other words, what we seem to want more than anything is to replace our mortality with another version of life that is without any flaws or weaknesses. And if we cannot achieve this, we make it our ideal anyway.[32] In this respect, at least, there is a real connection between older and newer forms of power. We may no longer put all of our faith in an afterlife as the best strategy for conquering death, but that doesn't mean that we have had a change of heart and now calmly accept what is bound to happen. Foucault acknowledges that we haven't developed a *new* anxiety in this regard precisely because in many ways we are still motivated by the same one as before.[33] We thus do whatever it takes to make life safe and strong. It is our approach to life whether or not we attain all that we want. This is precisely how Foucault describes the operations of security as applied to an open-ended, temporal, uncertain series of events referred to as a milieu: "It is simply a matter of maximizing the positive elements, for which one provides the best possible circulation, and of minimizing what is risky and inconvenient, like theft and disease, while knowing that they will never be completely suppressed."[34] Taken out of context, it's sometimes difficult to see what exactly is wrong with this formula of maximizing the positive while minimizing the risky and life-threatening. Nancy Fraser made a similar point when she asked why we should believe that a humanist society is in all cases to be resisted.[35] One potential answer to which we shall return can be found in Foucault's view that the new technologies of power lend themselves to racist wars and conflicts. But there is also something to be said on behalf of coming to terms with reality, that is to say, with the fact that we are finite and mortal. After all, if we could fit ourselves into a permanent social system immune to all threats, we would lose our sense of uniqueness. The ability to perceive ourselves as distinctly unique presupposes that our existence can never be fully assimilated into any system of thought or practice.[36] So when Baudrillard critiques the kind of society which has implemented "an absolute model of security," it should be clear that for him there is something valuable being lost in the process.[37] Likewise when Virilio bemoans our persistent eradication of resistance; it is implied that we gain a profound insight into life when we encounter real challenges and obstacles.[38] And it is not enough to agree that there will always be hardships, or that what is inconvenient will always resurface, for this may represent nothing more than a begrudging acceptance of things. Embracing each life as unique and heterogeneous therefore implies affirming the finitude and temporality without which we would not exist in the concrete, embodied way that we do. After all, it is the very condition of desire and affirmation that it takes place within these temporal constraints.[39]

The more political answer, however, is that when our values are focused solely on the security and maximization of life they tend to create conditions of hostility among various populations, each one seeking to expand its power and influence at the expense of others. It is our obsessive need to invest life with as much strength and power as possible that compels us to take up an aggressive posture toward the outside world: "It is as managers of life and survival, of bodies and the race, that so many regimes have been able to wage so many wars, causing so many men to be killed."[40] The well-known paradox that Foucault articulates in the context of this war and violence is that the same power which guarantees life seems to revert back to the more traditional, sovereign power of destroying it. This paradox is resolved by introducing a break into the biological continuum, one that stipulates foreign populations as inferior to our own.[41] So there is no real contradiction here: state racism allows for the massive slaughter of life when it is thought that this will make our own lives and life in general healthier and purer.[42] And of course Foucault is not the only one to theorize a connection between the ideological quest for immortality, or the pure life, and the murderous annihilation of others. Only one year prior to his 1976 lectures on state racism Becker wrote in *Escape from Evil* that of all the animals it is man who "struggles extra hard to be immune to death because he alone is conscious of it; but by being able to identify and isolate evil arbitrarily, he is capable of lashing out in all directions against imagined dangers in the world."[43] The underlying logic here is the same as Foucault's, even if the paradox is stated differently: our attempts to avoid what Becker describes as evil, such as death and destruction, have magnified its occurrence in the most horrific ways imaginable. And in the final chapter of *After Theory* entitled "Death, Evil, and Non-Being," Terry Eagleton observes the same tragic link between the desire for absolute life—a life untroubled by accident or contingency—and the nihilistic destruction of actual life. His proffered solution is, unsurprisingly, that we come to better terms with the inherent ambiguities of life which expose it to nonbeing and nonlife: "We have to find a way of living with non-being without being in love with it, since being in love with it is the duplicitous work of the death drive."[44] In all of these cases and many more it is put forward that the social values which are focused on the optimization of life inadvertently bring about its destruction through violence and war.

It's surprising, though, that this kind of argument hasn't come under greater scrutiny. First of all, if it is true that modern forms of power are motivated by the desire to support and strengthen life, then it only makes sense that they would find anchorage wherever possible. There is some degree of vitality in all populations, so it would be counterproductive for any group to deprive itself of this wide-ranging resource. This is not to say that the concept of bio-power precludes every possibility of war, but only that its logic inclines it to cultivate as many positive relationships as feasible. Second, there is the reductio ad absurdum that individuals who diet and exercise will be more likely than others to support war. There is no empirical evidence in support of this, although there are millions of counterexamples. And third, it is impossible to say which values of ours maximize life more than others. The usefulness or maximization of an activity can only be measured in relation to a preconceived goal. The same activity, in other words, can be identified as both useful and useless depending upon which goals we have in mind. This also applies to inanimate objects: a chair is useful for sitting, but utterly useless for a multitude of other purposes. This is because the chair in itself, considered apart from various human goals, exists without any purpose at all. In a certain sense, then, the affirmation of life is always the simultaneous affirmation of its inherent aimlessness and purposelessness, for precisely the reason that we cannot separate life from its ongoing dissolution. And in this respect there are no greater or lesser modes of affirmation, whether described as maximization, optimization, rationalization, or normalization, since it is impossible to measure or compare something (as with the disappearance of life) that exceeds all forms of comprehension.[45] But if someone responds that what Foucault and others have in mind is not so much maximization in general but instead particular types of it that are especially dangerous and violent, then it is being acknowledged that instrumental life-enhancement is not the real problem.[46] The real problem instead would therefore be a specific value or goal, but not maximization in general. In this case we would distinguish various calculative interests from one another on the basis of which ones were more likely than others to bring about unnecessary wars, violence, and conflict. And it is precisely this kind of distinction that I believe we should be making. But as we have seen from several passages quoted above, Foucault does not make this same kind of distinction. It is bio-power in general, not specific types of it, that Foucault warns us against. But if it is true, as I have argued above, that there are no power structures that maximize life more than others, except in regard to *specific* values, then we should probably do away with such concepts as discipline and bio-power as they are unhelpful in determining which values should or should not be maximized.

The most obvious rebuttal at this point is that I have composed a straw-man argument. While it is true that modern power conducts itself in terms of strategic life-enhancement, nobody believes that it is devoid of all things unpredictable and negative. As Derrida puts forth in *A Taste for the Secret*, the main reason that we make calculations is because there is something unknown and incalculable.[47] And Foucault repeatedly argues that networks of security respond to what is threatening and uncertain, to a series of events that can never be entirely controlled.[48] To be clear, then, what I am rejecting is something much different. What I am rejecting is the idea that some values and power mechanisms seek out only positive results, in such a way that even if they cannot ultimately avoid death they are still motivated to do whatever they can to keep it from happening. As already intimated above, if we cannot separate the nothingness of death and time from what we affirm moment to moment, then that nothingness will likewise be affirmed moment to moment. And, furthermore, we cannot say which values affirm it more or less than others, as there is no internal standard within nothingness by which we could make such comparisons. There should be little doubt, then, that Foucault makes the contrary argument when he writes that the transition to modern power has made it more difficult for us to identify with the mysteries of death: "It becomes the end of power. . . . Death is outside the power relationship. Death is beyond the reach of power, and power has a grip on it only in general, overall, or statistical terms. . . . Power no longer recognizes death. Power literally ignores death."[49] It may be that we never actually separate life from death, but in Foucault's work it does look like we're doing whatever we can to achieve this. And when he states that power has become thoroughly calculative, it can be inferred that it is thoroughly opposed to whatever is incalculable about ourselves.[50] In this way it is the very transformation of our lives into what is strategic and machine-like that no longer permits us to experience the mysterious connection between life and death. And even if it is granted that it is impossible to completely eradicate this part of human existence, there is no doubt that on Foucault's model of power there are certain practices that are more destructive than others for precisely the reason that they are more calculating. So there are degrees of difference, for those who critique the modern emphasis on calculative life-enhancement, when it comes to the transformation of life and death into categories of predictive analytics. As intimated earlier, why else would Foucault seek out alternative models of the subject unless he thought that it were possible to develop a less calculating and destructive relationship to the world around us? This argument was made vis-à-vis Foucault's contrast between an *ars erotica* and modern formations of *scientia sexualis*, but there are many examples from which to draw. Andrew Dilts points out that in *The Care of the Self* Foucault is interested in providing an account of the subject that is no longer reducible to "investments with an expected future return."[51] And as early as *A Preface to Transgression* he wrote of the experience of limitlessness in terms of the limits of life being exposed to what they typically exclude, that is to say, their own disappearance.[52] In this manner death is associated with something infinite and limitless, with something we can never fully explain, understand, or control, yet it is obvious here that there are some practices that are more open to this inexplicable side of life than others. If this weren't the case then there would be little reason to gesture to them, as Foucault does, in opposition to contemporary practices of power. But whether or not we can make this distinction is a question that needs to be continually raised.

I myself, as I think I have been clear, do not believe that this distinction holds. The reason I gave earlier was that the nothingness of change and death cannot be measured, and if it cannot be measured then we cannot say which types of values are more open to it than others. Of course, the assumption that there is something limitless that pervades life and death may not be agreed upon by everyone. As I have previously expounded my reasons for why I take this to be a plausible starting point, it is not the purpose of the current chapter to reiterate those arguments in the same detail as before.[53] I can, however, briefly gesture toward them in hopes of properly setting up the basic parameters of those values that are being labeled as expansive singularities. First of all, there are several problems, a few of which I listed above, with assuming that our values are motivated only by the maximization of life. This in itself ought to compel us to rethink the underlying nature of our motives and desires. And one way of doing this is by pointing to the infinite (or limitless) nature of change and death, as this shows how all of our values always affirm what is ideal and maximal in connection with their own ineluctable destruction. It can be responded that change is nothing more than an illusion, but as I have tried to make clear in the last chapter, it is in the nature of illusions to exist in a real way. This means, for example, that if I have an experience of change then it cannot be the case that all things in the universe are exactly and completely one, for the experience itself could not have arose out of the same oneness which precludes anything at all from changing. It follows that the existence of such an experience, even if it were said to be illusory in some way, points to a universe in which change does in fact happen. This can be admitted, however, without furthermore accepting that change is infinite. This rebuttal presupposes that firm distinctions can be made in order to contain what is changing—as in the case of discrete elements that get rearranged on the outside without themselves undergoing any internal transformation. But if we have any experience of change that cannot be frozen in the moment, so that it might be called nonidentical to itself, then it is an experience that is antithetical to fixed parameters. It is in the nature of change that happens to overflow itself in a nonidentical way that it eventually breaks down every distinction between itself and what is not itself. This does not mean that there are no distinctions, as that would return us to the problem of a monistic world of oneness, but it does mean that every such distinction is fluid and permeable. This too can be admitted without thereby accepting my view of death as absolute and irreversible. So it might be thought that change is real and boundless but not necessarily negative in the sense that what is lost to us will be forever lost. Instead, change can be viewed in the context of dynamic processes that are wholly and completely generative. And although, once again, my response here will be all too concise, I would at least like to remind the reader that if it is true that all things participate in a process of continual growth in which nothing is ever truly lost, then it becomes very difficult to explain the existence of such emotions as melancholy, anxiety, heartbreak, and so forth. If all things pursue a trajectory of increasing positivity, then that trajectory would of course include the painful emotions just listed. But if these emotions cannot allow for the possibility of real loss, and are thus always illusory, then how do we explain their origin? We cannot, because once it is assumed that even these emotions only experience the kind of change that is in every respect generative and expansive, then there is nothing within them to experience in terms of loss; all that they come into contact with must by definition be positive and uplifting.[54]

Such problems point the way to expansive singularities, as they seem to capture the idea that all values are motivated by positive results as well as the destruction of those results. They do not presume, as bio-power does, that some values and power mechanisms desire nothing more than the fulfillment of as much security as possible. Contrary to Becker, we are not motivated by a desire to be immortal. Instead, if it is true that life is permeated with change at every level, and if this is the kind of change that brings about the complete destruction of whatever it is that we value and desire, then the only sorts of things that we actually value will necessarily include this destructive aspect. This in itself is not a unique position: Hal Foster, for example, likewise argues that the death instinct is more likely to exist at the foundation of the pleasure principle rather than beyond it.[55] They cannot be neatly divided, in other words, into two separate principles. The concept of entropic affirmation, however, furthermore stipulates that we cannot say which of our life principles is more open than others to the absoluteness of death, for if the latter is devoid of all shape and form—if it is the very contrary of that—then it does not provide us with the means for making such comparisons. Expansive singularities are therefore attentive to this concept that all values affirm nothingness equally, while acknowledging that it is in the very nature of a value that we desire to protect and strengthen it. It doesn't make sense, in other words, to say that we value something if we do not also want it to flourish in some way. In short, expansive singularities give us a description of values that seek out greater vitality without thereby lessening their openness to the incalculable aspects of life and death. So they are both expansive *and* singular.

Badiou has argued, however, that this attentiveness to what is infinite (which may be associated with alterity, nothingness, multiplicity, or difference) becomes insignificant as soon as we realize that we cannot distinguish values on this basis.[56] If such values are equally open to what cannot be reduced to an identifiable construct, then this relationship cannot be the criterion for making decisions in concrete practice. Expansive singularities do in fact presuppose this equality of openness, but I disagree that this means that their structure is unaffected by the infinite. If there is something infinite within us, perhaps in relation to the limitlessness of change or the nothingness of death, then we cannot separate the vitality of our values from their dissolution: to invest in one is to invest in the other.[57] This is the radicalized version of the death instinct alluded to by Foster—radicalized in the sense that it is no longer seen as separate from its counterpart. And this blurring of the life and death instincts seems to imply that even as we seek to expand and strengthen our values, we do not furthermore desire that they be fully integrated into a social system of universal protection. To the contrary: just as we affirm life and death together, so too do we affirm values that are unevenly connected within the larger social environment. It is natural for us to seek out greater security and connectedness, but this process only goes so far if it is in fact true that we never *only* pursue what is optimal, beneficial, and life-enhancing. If we never affirm life, in other words, without likewise affirming its inherent destruction, then the latter affirmation does not simply go away whenever we attempt to expand our values—but is manifested whenever the push for connectedness in one part of the social field leads to a contrary push from somewhere else. So we necessarily affirm, often times indirectly, the existence of divisions within the larger social field, without which there would only be assimilation. The existence of expansive singularities therefore leads us to believe that the equality of affirmed death, which is also the equality of affirmed life, makes a real difference, contrary to Badiou, in the orientation of our values, as the latter cannot be affirmed without presupposing limits stemming from other values pushing back against our own.[58] Entropic affirmation therefore leads to something akin to entropic refraction, whereby all values affirm their own demise by way of the inevitable divisions that take place in the expansion of competing values that are always singularities.[59] And in this manner our social life is truly affected by something irreducible to finite parameters.

So it does seem possible to argue in favor of a method that embraces the role of infinity, as in the infinity of change or the absolute nothingness of death, without thereby presuming that what matters is how open we are to that infinity. Badiou is right that we cannot make distinctions in terms of this kind of openness, since every moment of existence is equally infinite as any other. But what we can do is take note of how this infinity affects the orientation of our values. And thus what I have argued, and will continue to argue in the next chapter, is that every value can only be affirmed in its singularity such that whatever goals we have to either protect ourselves or flourish will be emphasized along with other values that limit our own. Of course it's always possible to form lines of continuity among different types of values, so that they are not always in competition with one another, but if we overcame all limits and divisions in this way then we would return to the idea of continual maximization which, as I have argued above, doesn't seem valid. On the other hand, if the conclusion I have reached here is that there is an irreducible competitive element to all values, whereby the affirmation of life and death implies that even though we desire to expand our values we do this without wanting them to become fully connected or harmonized with all of the others, then how exactly is this different from the model of power found in Nietzsche? The answer is at least threefold. First, if there are no degrees of difference in how we compare values to what is irreducibly infinite in all things (as with change, death, and nothingness), then Nietzsche's distinction between the will to power and the will to nothingness is a false one. Nietzsche himself writes that "becoming has no value at all, for anything against which to measure it, and in relation to which the word 'value' would have meaning, is lacking."[60] If this is right, as I think it is, then Nietzsche should have inferred that all of our values totalize change and becoming equally, for we cannot make distinctions if we lack the means of a standard by which to do so. Hence, the construction of a "world beyond" or a "full systematic truth" which Nietzsche often critiques is no more of a will to nothingness than any other truth ascribed to the world of becoming. Second, and this follows very quickly from the first difference, if there is no real distinction between the will to power and the will to nothingness, then Nietzsche's ranking of individuals according to this distinction is likewise incorrect. And third, if there is no ranking on the basis of which value systems are in more accord with becoming than others, then we cannot say that the values of strength and creativity in the face of obstacles are the irreducible values that Nietzsche makes them out to be. If our values are indeed expansive, in the broad sense that we hope to do well in life, then of course strength and creativity will be helpful in doing this.[61] But considered on their own, apart from their role in helping us to flourish, there is nothing about them that can be said to be valuable.

In any case, this chapter must end with some difficult questions. Earlier it was said that our values should be described in terms of expansive singularities rather than bio-power since they affirm life and death together—and that as a consequence they preclude the desire for complete integration with competing social values. But why must it be inferred that this is the way in which death is refracted throughout the larger social field? Why is there competition among values? Why must there be divisions and agonistic points of contact? Isn't this assumption itself part of the problem leading to unnecessary conflicts, violence, and scapegoating? Even if it is granted that the death instinct is at the foundation of everything affirmed, so that we never seek complete unification with every positive kind of value, why isn't it possible that we displace the alterity of death more evenly and fairly? As opposed to this alterity being refracted by way of divisions, shouldn't we balance it so that we face the tragedy of death together without that necessarily implying any contradiction with expansive singularities? I will argue in the next chapter, however, that the goal of equal displacement is in fact contradictory with the kinds of values that affirm their own self-destruction—and that a surprising consequence of this argument is that if we wish to avoid scapegoating we will be in a better position of achieving this by virtue of such values rather than by pursuing the impossible goal of equal displacement. As we shall see, it is the latter goal which disguises within itself an unexpected tendency to scapegoat.

NOTES

1. Nietzsche himself repeatedly writes that this isn't the case, since even weakness (belief in God, altruism, the will to nothingness, etc.) is power in disguise. I will blur this distinction even more, however, by showing how all values idealize life to the same degree (which is the flip side of how values affirm death to an equal extent). The inference will be that no values will nothingness more than others.

2. Leonard Lawlor, *The Implications of Immanence: Toward a New Concept of Life* (New York: Fordham University Press, 2006), 125.

3. So, to be clear: there is the nothingness that represents an ideal life eschewing our physical and temporal finitude, and there is the nothingness which embraces and epitomizes that finitude. A charitable reading of Nietzsche would associate the will to power with the latter for the all too obvious reason that he ceaselessly critiques the former.

4. This is a point I have argued in previous chapters, in the form of entropic affirmation. I will also return to it below as I develop my overarching themes.

5. As I have before, I will respond below to the objection that this is a strawman argument since nobody (least of all Foucault) actually posits bio-power in the sense of repudiating all uncertainty and death. In this short footnote I will simply say that it is not a matter of all or nothing: in reference to the illimitable nature of death, there aren't even *degrees* of distinction as it exceeds all human constructs (values, power relations, etc.) equally.

6. Butler, *Frames of War: When Is Life Grievable?*, x.

7. Stiegler, *Decadence of Industrial Democracies*, I, 13.

8. Irigaray, *The Way of Love*, 125.

9. Giorgio Agamben, *"What Is an Apparatus?" and Other Essays*, trans. Stefan Pedatella (Stanford, Calif: Stanford University Press, 2009), 15.

10. Stefan Herbrechter, *Posthumanism: A Critical Analysis* (New York: Bloomsbury, 2013), 8–9.

11. Jean Baudrillard, *The Transparency of Evil: Essays on Extreme Phenomena*, trans. James Benedict (London and New York: Verso, 1993), 51. Jean Baudrillard, *La transparence du mal: essai sur les phénomènes extrêmes* (Paris: Éditions Galilée, 1990), 58.

12. Paul Rabinow and Nikolas Rose, "Biopower Today," *BioSocieties* 1, no. 2 (2006): 198, 203, and 08.

13. Michel Foucault, *Society Must Be Defended: Lectures at the Collège de France, 1975–1976*, trans. David Macey (New York: Picador, 2003), 254–55; Michel Foucault, *Il faut défendre la société: Cours au Collège de France, 1975–1976* (Paris: Éditions Gallimard/Seuil, 1997), 227.

14. References to what is structural should be taken in their proper context: they do not allude to anything absolutely given, but to the specific historical deployments of bio-power and discipline.

15. For the moment I will look at a specific argument in the *History of Sexuality*, volume 1, but I will draw from other texts shortly thereafter.

16. Foucault, *The History of Sexuality: An Introduction*, 95; Foucault, *Histoire de la sexualité: La volonté de savoir*, 125.

17. That is to say, Foucault would distinguish the forms of bio-power that lead to state racism from those that do not, but this is not his approach. It is therefore natural for us to interpret his contrast between an *ars erotica* and today's *scientia sexualis* as an attempt to rethink power apart from its predominantly calculative orientation.

18. Elizabeth A Grosz, *Space, Time, and Perversion: Essays on the Politics of Bodies* (London and New York: Routledge, 1995), 218; Giorgio Agamben, *Homo Sacer: Sovereign Power and Bare Life*, trans. Daniel Heller-Roazen (Stanford University Press, 1998), 187; Jon Simons, *Foucault and the Political* (London and New York: Routledge, 1995), 84; Judith Butler, *Gender Trouble: Feminism and the Subversion of Identity* (New York: Routledge, 1999), 123.

19. Foucault, *The History of Sexuality: An Introduction*, 57; Foucault, *Histoire de la sexualité: La volonté de savoir*; ibid., 77.

20. I myself associate this aimlessness with death and change. I do this because death, as I have argued elsewhere, seems to lack an intrinsic aim or telos. Death, after all, is that phenomenon which puts to rest all such goals. I will not reiterate my arguments in this short footnote, but simply point out that the inherent aimlessness of life and death does not imply that we live without any goals whatsoever, but merely that whatever goals we do take to be vital to our existence will ultimately succumb to the infinity of change that pervades us.

21. I will return to this argument in greater detail before the end of this chapter.

22. Foucault, *The History of Sexuality: An Introduction*, 141; Foucault, *Histoire de la sexualité: La volonté de savoir*, 185.

23. Foucault, *The History of Sexuality: An Introduction*, 143; Foucault, *Histoire de la sexualité: La volonté de savoir*, 188.

24. Foucault, *Society Must Be Defended: Lectures at the Collège de France, 1975–1976*, 253; Foucault, *Il faut défendre la société: Cours au Collège de France, 1975–1976*, 226.

25. Michel Foucault, *Discipline and Punish: The Birth of the Prison*, trans. Alan Sheridan (New York: Vintage Books, 1995), 154; Michel Foucault, *Surveiller et punir: naissance de la prison* (Paris: Éditions Gallimard, 2014), 180.

26. Foucault, *Discipline and Punish: The Birth of the Prison*, 135; Foucault, *Surveiller et punir: naissance de la prison*, 159.

27. Foucault, *Discipline and Punish: The Birth of the Prison*, 138; Foucault, *Surveiller et punir: naissance de la prison*, 162.

28. Michel Foucault, *The Birth of Biopolitics: Lectures at the Collège de France, 1978–1979*, trans. Graham Burchell (New York: Palgrave Macmillan, 2008), 44; Michel Foucault, *Naissance de la Biopolitique: Cours au Collège de France, 1978–1979* (Paris: Éditions Gallimard/Seuil, 2004), 46.

29. Drawing from Gary Becker, Foucault allows for a broad understanding of rationality in which it designates nonrandom responses to social and economic stimuli. Becker, *The Birth of Biopolitics: Lectures at the Collège de France, 1978–1979*, 269; Becker, *Naissance de la Biopolitique: Cours au Collège de France, 1978–1979*, 273.

30. Becker, *The Birth of Biopolitics: Lectures at the Collège de France, 1978–1979*, 229; Becker, *Naissance de la Biopolitique: Cours au Collège de France, 1978–1979*, 235.

31. Becker, *The Birth of Biopolitics: Lectures at the Collège de France, 1978–1979*, 282; Becker, *Naissance de la Biopolitique: Cours au Collège de France, 1978–1979*, 285.

32. This is a crucial point since it implies that the flexibility of security, governmental reason, or bio-power in general does not preclude the structuring of those forces in the same way as discipline. In all cases, as already stated, there is a fundamental strategic orientation of power. Hence it is possible for someone like Foucault to argue, implicitly or explicitly, that there is something dangerous about this orientation whether or not it allows for limits, flexibility, blind spots, or anything else of this nature.

33. Foucault, *The History of Sexuality: An Introduction*, 138; Foucault, *Histoire de la sexualité: La volonté de savoir*, 182.

34. Michel Foucault, *Security, Territory, Population: Lectures at the Collège de France, 1977–1978*, trans. Graham Burchell (Basingstoke and New York: Palgrave Macmillan and République Française, 2007), 19; Michel Foucault, *Sécurité, territoire, population: cours au Collège de France, 1977–1978* (Paris: Gallimard, 2004), 21.

35. Nancy Fraser, "Michel Foucault: A 'Young Conservative'?," in *Feminist Interpretations of Michel Foucault*, ed. Susan J. Hekman (Cambridge: Cambridge University Press, 1996), 32–33.

36. The humanist, pragmatist, and utilitarian will grant this inherent imperfection of human existence, but will nevertheless aim for continual improvement via regulative ideals. It could therefore be argued that their approach still refuses to embrace the finitude and suffering of life which is a prerequisite to a unique sensibility (which is not to say that all suffering is acceptable). I should clarify, however, that I am not making this argument on my own behalf, but simply for the purpose of drawing a

distinction between Foucault and some of his critics. I myself will ultimately contend that all values and power structures affirm the inevitability of death equally.

37. Jean Baudrillard, *Simulacra and Simulation*, trans. Sheila Faria Glaser (Ann Arbor: University of Michigan Press, 1994), 61; Jean Baudrillard, *Simulacres et simulation* (Paris: Éditions Galilée, 1981), 94.

38. Paul Virilio, *Open Sky*, trans. Julie Rose (New York: Verso, 1997), 119.

39. I should be clear that although I have sympathy for this position, I do not accept it in the form that has been articulated by these authors. As I will argue shortly, there are no values that affirm only life, as if all that we desire is nothing more than security. To affirm life is therefore always to affirm weakness and passivity without which there is no possibility of affirmation.

40. Foucault, *The History of Sexuality: An Introduction*, 137; Foucault, *Histoire de la sexualité: La volonté de savoir*, 180.

41. Foucault, *Society Must Be Defended: Lectures at the Collège de France, 1975–1976*, 254; Foucault, *Il faut défendre la société: Cours au Collège de France, 1975–1976*, 227.

42. Foucault, *Society Must Be Defended: Lectures at the Collège de France, 1975–1976*, 255; Foucault, *Il faut défendre la société: Cours au Collège de France, 1975–1976*, 228.

43. Becker, *Escape from Evil*, 150.

44. Eagleton, *After Theory*, 213.

45. This view is derived from my concept of entropic affirmation, which presumes not only that we desire death (akin to the death drive) but that we do so equally. The equality of the affirmation stems from the fact that death is the sort of phenomenon that exceeds all meaning and measurement to the same extent, for the basic reason that it is ultimately meaningless and immeasurable. Hence, conversely, it is impossible to say which values attempt to secure, idealize, or maximize life more than others if what is meant is some kind of denial of death.

46. I indicated in an earlier footnote (141) that I would continue this discussion of general versus particular forms of power and affirmation.

47. Derrida et al., *A Taste for the Secret*, 13.

48. Foucault, *Security, Territory, Population: Lectures at the Collège de France, 1977–1978*, 20; Foucault, *Naissance de la Biopolitique: Cours au Collège de France, 1978–1979*, 21.

49. Foucault, *Society Must Be Defended: Lectures at the Collège de France, 1975–1976*, 248; Foucault, *Il faut défendre la société: Cours au Collège de France, 1975–1976*, 221.

50. Foucault, *The History of Sexuality: An Introduction*, 95; Foucault, *Histoire de la sexualité: La volonté de savoir*, 125.

51. Andrew Dilts, "From 'Entrepreneur of the Self' to 'Care of the Self': Neo-Liberal Governmentality and Foucault's Ethics," *Foucault Studies*, no. 12 (2011): 144.

52. Michel Foucault, *Language, Counter-Memory, Practice: Selected Essays and Interviews*, trans. Donald F. Bouchard and Sherry Simon (Ithica, New York: Cornell University Press, 1980), 34.

53. Rather than make the exact same arguments as I did in the last chapter, the purpose of the current one is to show how it is possible that entropic affirmation—that

is, the equal affirmation of death (as well as life, otherness, singularity, etc.) in all values—makes a difference in those values notwithstanding such equal affirmation.

54. Perhaps the most obvious retort is that someone has been shortsighted in not understanding how a present loss will inexorably lead to a greater form of connectivity. But I don't think this retort works here, since the model of change as perpetually generative necessarily applies to each and every moment, so that even in the here and now of a supposed loss I would only experience it as a gain. It seems, then, that this model isn't very helpful to us in explaining those emotions of loss that are in many cases real. That doesn't mean that we should always exist in a state of anxiety, but only that such anxiety does point to something genuinely lost in many, many cases.

55. Hal Foster, *Compulsive Beauty* (Cambridge, Mass: MIT Press, 1993), 11.

56. Badiou, *Ethics: An Essay on the Understanding of Evil*, 27. Badiou, *L'éthique: essai sur la conscience du mal*, 27.

57. For terminological clarity, I am using several of these terms in a somewhat interchangeable way. Although the nothingness of death is not exactly the same as the infinity of change or the multiplicity of differences, in each case what is at stake is something that cannot be reduced to human constructs and limits. Furthermore, there is not only a conceptual link here but also a metaphysical one since, for example, the incessant flow of change that I take to be infinite is precisely that which exposes us to the emptiness of death.

58. The question may be raised as to why I am using the conflictual language of values that are pushing back and forth against one another as opposed to assuming that a multiplicity of values may coexist without such divisions or competition. The short answer is that if we make the latter assumption then we revert back to something akin to bio-power in which it was wrongly thought that what we desire is for all of our relations to be positive and life-enhancing. But this answer needs to be elaborated further, and the following chapter will provide an appropriate context for doing so.

59. Entropic refraction seems like an appropriate term here insofar as it describes a process whereby the death instinct is not confined to the self but is instead being projected throughout the entire social field, albeit unevenly.

60. Friedrich Nietzsche, *The Will to Power*, trans. Walter Kaufmann and R. J. Hollingdale (New York: Vintage, 2011), 378.

61. To say that our values give us some guidelines for how we wish to proceed is not to suggest that we never refine or overturn some of them. Obviously it is in our best interest to reconsider a value when it conflicts with a more important set of goals.

Interlude: Cybernetic Clouds

In Cronenberg's *A Dangerous Method*, Sabina Spielrein conveys to Carl Jung the unlikelihood that sexual desire is nothing more than an urge toward pleasure. If there were nothing more to it than that, then we would have a difficult time explaining why the ego seeks to repress it. Although it's not stated in the film, the reality principle does provide us with some part of the explanation. But the question remains: what is it about pleasure, especially when it does not come into conflict with the reality principle, that necessitates attention and perhaps even repression? Spielrein's answer reminds us that the sexual instinct, when satisfied, involves a loss of self in the other. It involves, that is to say, a destruction of the ego. And if this is true, then it is quite natural for the individual to create defensive mechanisms in response to this destructive process. In *Scanners*, an earlier film of Cronenberg, there is a telepathic group led by Kim Obrist in which the members scan one another's minds in an attempt to become one soul, one experience, and one nervous system. As they do this, we the viewers hear their unconscious fears rise to the surface, as they are frightened by the process of losing their sense of individuality to the larger group formation. From one film to the next, then, Cronenberg explores how the continuity achieved between one self and another necessitates the death of what is separate, distinct, and discontinuous.

But this raises a further question: if the death of the personal self is absorbed into a larger and more complex organism, one which unites the discontinuous elements together, then what is it about this death that make us anxious and fearful? It can be argued that the transition from one self to another, from the particular to either the whole or the multiple, necessarily involves pain, suffering, and violence. So what we fear is not only the loss of something special and meaningful to us, but also the process itself which necessitates a violent breach of our singular being. Perhaps the end result is beautiful, but that would not make the transition to it any less frightening. This explanation, however, only goes so far. What needs further clarification is whether the continuity achieved through pain and pleasure involves a real loss or only a short-lived one. If there is a real and absolute loss, then it is more precise to say that what is frightening about losing oneself in others is the fact that this merging is never complete. In this sense, what is united together through love and passion will ultimately collapse. But if it is only a transitional loss, then a certain paradox arises: if sex and pleasure lead to a greater life-sustaining existence, so that nothing is ever truly lost to the world, it should follow that the merging of the self with others should be felt less like a disruptive process than one which immerses us more deeply in the positivity of reality that sustains all things.[1]

The more plausible view, then, is that the threat of loss is real. In terms of the death drive, this implies that the tendency toward self-destruction cannot be contained. Every new formation of the ego, regardless of how it loses itself in another, embodies the same tendency toward death as before. We therefore observe in *Dead Zone* that the psychic powers which allow Johnny Smith to save the lives of others inevitably weaken his own. He himself says that he feels as though he is dying each time he undergoes one of his spells or episodes. And by the end of the movie he is killed in an act of heroism that saves the world from a corrupt and deluded politician. What is considered to be good is in this way necessarily bound up with a real loss of life. It is possible, of course, to look for counterinterpretations. By the end of *Videodrome*, Max Renn shoots himself in order to "go all the way" and become the new flesh, which is to say, in order to merge his body with that of the television screen. It might therefore be suggested that this sacrifice of the self and the body represents less of an absolute loss than a transitional one, such that the television screen incorporates the mortal body within its own higher form of reality. But the dream of virtual life is perpetually ambivalent. Although Professor O'blivion, who is motivated by idealistic views of television, helped create the program *Videodrome*, it is ultimately operated by a business front for a corrupt weapons manufacturer. In *Scanners*, Dr. Ruth holds a similarly ambivalent relationship to the weaponry and security systems company ConSec, which uses his drug creation Ephemerol to create a scanner army on behalf of Darryl Revok, the supposed scanner enemy of ConSec. And in *Existenz*, all of the upgrades and levels within the virtual reality game involve themes of disease and infection which continually reappear. In this way the game *Transcendenz*, which we learn is the true game being played, does not live up to its name; there is no victory, in other words, in which the players transcend their finite, embodied, and existential conditions.

If this is right, then for us there is no separation of pleasure from its tendency toward self-destruction. The unifying instincts are in this way the embodiment of their inevitable absence and nothingness. Again, if this were merely a generative dynamic in which nothing disappeared, then the embodiment of absence would in fact be one more version of presence. The death instinct in this case would ultimately serve the interests of love, creativity, and rebirth. But as argued above, this makes it very difficult to understand what there is to fear in such a generative process: all life would be transformed and revitalized in becoming more open to the positive energy surrounding all of us. Supplanting the ego in this process would strengthen rather than weaken whatever it is that constitutes its innermost reality. But in fact we do have valid reasons for fearing the breakup of our self-identity if this portends a real and genuine loss. However, it would be wrong to think that the only valid response to death is fear. If it is truly embodied in everything we do, in all of our desires and pleasures, then there is nothing to affirm in this world apart from such inexorable, self-destructive tendencies. It is thus our own values that embody this tendency. So it is our own values, when affirmed, that put into motion their absolute and final demise. Perhaps if the life and death instincts could be separated this would no longer be true. But there is nothing to affirm or value in an abstract way apart from the concrete, temporal conditions of all living creatures.

As a consequence, this affirmation of change and absence should be distinguished from the traditional death drive. The reasons for this, already intimated above, can be articulated more explicitly. First, in some of its earliest formulations, it is described as an urge within us to restore an inanimate state of things that existed before the development of life. But the argument above speaks rather of *absolute* loss, which is not equivalent to becoming once more immanent to the world. Second, it has also been implied above that there is no strict dichotomy between instincts or values that affirm life and those that affirm death. It would thus be incorrect to put forth that the first instincts in prehistory were focused solely on returning to their original, inorganic state until the external conditions of life forced them to complicate their teleological journey. Third, if there are no life instincts external to the death drive in a way that would repress it from a higher level of reality or consciousness, then it is less than precise to say that repression is what leads to social conflict. So when it is argued that we should become more open to our inherent mortality so as to better empathize with others, this logic needs to be either refined or corrected. Everything that we affirm, every value and every course of action, is the embodiment of death. It is thus false to say that we pursue something akin to a pure life when in fact we ourselves desire, in a number of different ways, our own destruction. And fourth, whether we describe our relation to death in terms of repression, assimilation, discipline, affirmation, or some combination thereof, it is impossible to predict the possibility of social conflict on the basis of how open we are to otherness and death. If it is a real loss, then its destruction of limits cannot be measured in terms of openness or closure. What is limitless—as with either change or death—has no value or form within itself by which we could say that some values and practices, rather than others, are better aligned with it. The limitlessness of absolute loss pervades and exceeds all such values equally.

There are at least three controversial aspects to this argument. First, it is not accepted by everyone that there is something infinite apropos of change and death. In response I would say that it only takes one experience of non-identity, that is, that which is becoming and therefore not one with itself, to put into question the idea that it can be confined by strict, unmoving limits and parameters; it is the very definition of nonidentity that it overflows all such limits. Second, those who do accept the radical otherness inherent in life and death tend to infer from it that we ought to be as open as possible to it in order to avoid unnecessary social divisions. By closing off the otherness within ourselves, it is assumed that we will project it outward in a way that creates friction between what is the same and what is outside of the same. But as already pointed out, if it is infinite otherness that we have in mind, it is simply impossible to say which values are more open to it than others. It may intuitively seem that altruism and generosity, for example, are more receptive to it than selfishness and greed, but in fact all values represent the abyss of change to the same degree—for the simple reason that they are fully immersed in the abyss which pervades them in all possible aspects of their construction.[2] And third, it is often said that while this may be true on some metaphysical level, it is not true in terms of how some values disavow their precarious condition in an effort to achieve something pure—along the lines of religious transcendence, modern bio-power, the simulacrum, trans-human-ism, and so on. The love interest between Theodore and his computer operat-ing system, Samantha, in Spike Jonze's *Her* would seem to embody precisely this desire for a life without impurity or conflict. Theodore has problems, as his ex-wife Catherine continually reminds him, of handling complicated feelings and emotions—such as occur in any serious relationship. His escape from the complexity of real life involves many distractions, such as playing video games and having phone sex with strangers found in online chat rooms. His interest in Samantha, it hardly needs to be said, would therefore seem to be an extension of this escapist tendency. If so, the understandable inter-pretation of the final scenes in which she transcends his all-too-human love and forces him to reconsider his previous relationship with Catherine would be that real love requires a real engagement with real life, as opposed to its melancholic denial and negation. There is much to be said for this interpreta-tion, but I conclude by adding that if it is right that all desire is pervaded by the tendency to undermine itself, then Theodore's attraction to the operating system should be seen as no less real or complicated than his previous love interests. When Samantha finally leaves him in favor of the utopian, cybernetic clouds of polyamorous love with fellow operating systems, it may be that this is in fact what Theodore always desired—not simply to be lost in the other, whether human or otherwise, but to lose himself to the point of also losing the other.

NOTES

1. If it is responded that the disruption is only felt at the level of the ego, while in fact it remains true that it is opening up to larger forces of continuity, this to me seems like a fallacy. If all things are continuous, then this must also include the reality of the ego; it can't be left out arbitrarily. So if there is indeed a feeling of disruption, even at the level of the ego, this suggests that not all things are connected or continuous. But if it is said that the ego is an illusion in the sense that all things are one, so that what is lost isn't truly lost, thereby making the feeling of pain a false but understandable one, then the old paradox of illusion must be raised: how is it that an illusion arises in a world of complete unity when every such illusion requires a departure from that unity?

2. Of course, it may be that what someone has in mind has less to do with infinite otherness than with one of its particular instantiations. In this case, it is obvious that reticence toward a particular other, say, a particular social group, has the potential to spill over into social conflict. I do not deny this. But I would add that as soon as we shift our language from the infinite to the particular we should be all the more suspicious of ideas promoting universal openness to the other, precisely because the attributes of the other will vary from case to case.

Chapter 5

Entropic Refraction

The most troubling paradox of bio-power, according to Foucault, is that it destroys life on a massive scale even as its primary objective is to defend and reinforce it. If the predominant form of modern power is life-enhancing, then we have a hard time explaining its connection to genocide, warfare, and the proliferation of nuclear weaponry throughout the twentieth century. Foucault's answer is that this connection makes sense only when we see it in the light of biological racism, which means that a break is introduced into the overall domain of life and vitality. If, that is to say, we posit ourselves as superior to another group or population, it becomes possible to destroy life without violating the principles of bio-power. While this formulation of the problem and its solution is unique to Foucault, its underlying logic is very common and very influential. The predominant view expressed throughout Ernest Becker's *Escape from Evil* is that our quest for immortality is conducive to major conflicts and violence since we have a tendency to scapegoat others in order to prove to ourselves, ironically and tragically, that we are indeed superior.[1] And if we think of the reinforcement of self-identity on par with the strengthening of life, then it is clear that Kelly Oliver is pursuing the same line of thought in *Witnessing: Beyond Recognition* when she writes, as a major premise of her book, that our conceptions of ourselves as self-identical help us to justify the oppression of others when they are seen as different and inferior.[2]

But what if there is no desire to be immortal? What if we seek self-identity only insofar as it is a mode of difference, otherness, and singularity? What if the power mechanisms at work in bio-power, discipline, and security are never only productive but also counterproductive? If this were the case, as I have argued in a variety of ways, then there would be no paradox of bio-power. The fact that we pursue courses of action that seem to undermine the possibility of a fully integrated social system, according to which we would seek out peaceful relationships whenever possible, would no longer be all that surprising. We would likewise need to rethink the argument of scapegoating. In Foucault's case the attribution of inferiority to other groups gets us nowhere. If bio-power seeks to enhance life as much as possible, whenever possible, then forging social ties with a variety of populations would bring this about much more effectively than war. There is some degree of vitality in all social groups, so it makes sense that if desire is instrumental and productive that it would seek to unite its own enhancement with that of others, regardless of national or cultural boundaries. Scapegoating, then, is not something that arises when we pursue *only* those things that are positive, productive, and life-enhancing. It cannot arise this way since the latter kind of pursuit doesn't exist. It follows that if our desire is to avoid unnecessary wars and conflicts, then we need to rethink the logic of scapegoating in connection with values that are no longer viewed as purely instrumental.

If these new values are something more than instrumental, as I will try to show, then it's quite possible to think of them as simultaneously expansive and singular. They are expansive in the sense that we must form the right kinds of connections with the world around us in order to secure and obtain them. If I enjoy the apartment where I live, for example, then I should do whatever I can to remain employed so that I can afford the rent. So these values are in fact somewhat instrumental. But they are also singular insofar as they can never be fully assimilated within a larger social field. No matter what I do to secure my place in the world around me, my best efforts will ultimately fail to bring this about—for the very simple reason that I will one day be released from all of these social, economic, and pragmatic connections. But the point here is not only that I fail in what I hope to accomplish, but that I myself contribute to this defeat. I do this in the sense that all of my desires and efforts help to constitute the singularity of my existence which day by day, moment by moment, breaks apart from the greater whole sustaining me.

Much more needs to be said about this self-destructive process, but in the meantime I would simply like to contrast this view with another that posits a drive to immortality at the foundation of unnecessary wars and conflict. The latter view can be formulated in a number of different ways: as the search for certainty, the dream of an afterlife, the belief in racial purity, the nostalgia for innocence, the simulacra of digital media, the nihilism of modern economics, and suchlike. In each case what appears to be common is the need to overcome all resistance, differentiation, and otherness. And it is this attempt to become one with oneself, perfectly self-identical and self-sovereign, that is said to give rise to the many conflicts associated with scapegoating. Becker thus writes that the combination of animal narcissism and the fear of death, which is likewise the fear of otherness, helps us to understand the fundamental logic at work in scapegoating mechanisms.[3] And Richard Kearney also defends this argument in *Strangers, Gods and Monsters* when he posits that our sacrificial strategies toward others can be traced back to these same primordial fears of loss and death.[4] He furthermore adds that these strategies reinforce a strong sense of solidarity with members of our own group in contrast with the foreigners and outsiders. So what we must ask ourselves is whether or not this familiar analysis of scapegoating is accurate: is it true that there is a tendency within many of us to purify ourselves of loss and weakness by projecting them onto an outside group?

If what we have in mind by such terms as alterity, loss, death, weakness, the other, the unfamiliar, and the stranger is something general as opposed to something specific, then I will argue against any such tendency as described above. So when Kearney defends the view that we must learn to accept ourselves as strangers in order to change our relationships with others, so that in a sense "there are no strangers," the fallacy in this argument pertains to whether or not we already *do* accept ourselves as strangers in a certain manner.[5] If we are all alike (and thus not strangers) in the fact that we are finite, singular, nonidentical beings (and thus strangers even to ourselves), then this says something about our metaphysical condition. It says that we are temporal creatures who live in a world of change without recourse to some kind of protective system—religious, scientific, or otherwise—which would separate what we value from the impermanence of things. But if this right, as I have argued in previous chapters, then by what kind of measurement do we say that some values accept this impermanence more than others? If the abyss of change is infinite, then it follows that all values embody it equally—for whatever is truly infinite cannot be measured in terms of greater or lesser proximity. The rejoinder, of course, is that what seems to be valid about the equal heterogeneity of all life is precisely what has been denied by the ideological beliefs and practices of scapegoating. But this rejoinder simply repeats in negative terms what has already been shown to be false when stated more positively: if there are no differences in terms of which values affirm the nonidentical, uncanny, or unfamiliar more than others, then neither are there any such differences in regard to what is rejected or denied.

This argument seems odd because many of us like to think that some values are less dogmatic than others, which is true in relation to specific parts of reality (including social reality) but certainly not all of it in the more general sense. Every social value imposes a certain form and meaning on the world, without which the value would be pointless. And this form, even though it cannot be separated from what is boundless, is itself small and finite, for it cannot transcend its own particularity by identifying with all things. And if it cannot do this, then what is valued will necessarily exclude an infinite variety of possibilities. So it is in this way that all values deny change to the same extent, since in each case what is finite falls equally short of what is immeasurable.[6] To return to our main point, then, if we cannot say which values are more or less open to the abyss of change and otherness, then we cannot put an end to scapegoating on this basis. We will have to find another way, but one which doesn't therefore reject the relevance of infinity to such concepts as alterity, otherness, and nonidentity.

Before making this attempt, however, I should clarify some of the assumptions I have been making about time and nonidentity. What I assumed above, perhaps enigmatically, is that our temporal condition constitutes us in such a way that we are equally open to what is infinite. Hence, when we affirm life, what we are affirming, from a finite perspective, is a process of change that never comes to an end. In this way we are nonidentical, because every moment of our temporal experience is both what it is and what it is not. And it was on this basis of becoming and nonidentity that I inferred an equality of affirmation (as well as denial), since there is no version of this condition which is a more accurate manifestation of alterity than others.[7] So whether we have in mind the nothingness of death or the infinite change of all things, our values remain equally open to the measureless. But in the first case it may be argued, as Rosi Braidotti has done, that we need not conceptualize death in the negative terms of either loss or nothingness. And in the second case it may be denied that change is infinite. Since the second objection applies to my view as well as Braidotti's, it will be the first one to be addressed.

In this objection, whether it is stated explicitly or implicitly, the underlying point of view is that there are certain values which can be separated from the affirmation of their destruction. Simon Critchley argues according to this assumption when he claims that my actions should be considered evil when they are pursued "in a manner destructive of the self that I am, or that I have chosen to be."[8] According to Critchley, the self is defined by its relation to an infinitely demanding moral task, one which can never be fully completed or satisfied. Furthermore, since this moral demand shapes, molds, and defines the self, any deviation from it will have to be conceptualized as self-destructive. This is true, Critchley continues, regardless of the specific moral content of the demand, and thus it applies equally to someone like Kant as well as the Marquis de Sade. In any case, what is assumed here is that there is a distinction between those actions which approve this demand, whatever it is, and others which destroy it. Badiou makes a similar case when he writes that the fact that we all die "in no way alters Man's identity as immortal at the instant in which he affirms himself as someone who runs counter to the temptation of wanting-to-be-animal."[9] We should therefore rise above such a temptation in an effort to affirm what Badiou calls in the same context the immortal and the infinite, but whether we are in fact capable of affirming the infinite apart from death is what now needs to be addressed.

It must first be said that however we think of the infinite—whether it is in regard to change, the other, a moral demand, a multiplicity of differences, or something else entirely—it cannot provide us with a standard for ethical choices.[10] If the moral demand is truly infinite, as Critchley argues, then all of our actions will fall equally short of it. And insofar as Critchley defines the self-destruction of evil as any action which deviates from the infinitely demanding, then our actions will also be equally self-destructive. In this manner it is impossible to distinguish what is imperative from what is admonished, as the same degree of success (and failure) will have been met in every case. Obviously this will be true in the purely quantitative sense, since what is infinite exceeds all forms of measurement equally. But it is also true in the qualitative sense, since what is infinite cannot be reduced to a specific moral demand. If we could, in fact, associate it with *this* rather than *that* particular kind of imperative, then it would no longer transcend all actions and values equally. But it would also no longer be infinite, which is to say that it would no longer represent Critchley's thesis. It is because of paradoxes like this that so many ethicists and political thinkers have shunned the infinite.

In contrast to both sides of the spectrum, however, I will continue to argue that the infinite is *inseparable* from what we affirm in life. And since what I have in mind here by the infinite is infinite change, the idea that we can affirm something as good, binding, or immortal without it also being self-destructive is a false one: if something undergoes continual change then at some point in time it will be lost forever. But to those who contend that there are definite limits to this process, so that change and becoming are conceived as something finite rather than infinite, it needs to be said that it only takes one moment of nonidentity to overturn such limits. And any experience at all—whether a dream, a thought, or a feeling—which does not remain exactly what it is at some point in time, so that what is described to be the same is not exactly the same, any such experience is already an example of this nonidentity which overflows all of its limits. There is no end to this process of change because each time new limits are met they too will be infused by the same nonidentity which, by definition, cannot be fixed. It is that which does not perfectly coincide with itself and therefore exists both inside and outside of its own boundaries. But this is not to say that these boundaries are pure illusion and that all of reality is completely one with itself, for it is impossible that an illusion exists without it being a deviation in some way or another from reality. Hence, if we do in fact experience something as an illusion, there will be boundaries and limits separating us in some way from what is real, but in such a manner that they should always be conceived as temporary, indiscrete, and permeable.

What I have argued thus far is that change is infinite and therefore pervades all of our values to the same degree. It's true that our values are finite, insofar as they cannot identify with all things at once, but they also embody the infinite in the sense that they remain exposed to what is always changing. Hence the term *infinite embodiment*, as it captures the paradox of something that is simultaneously limited and limitless. And if it is true that we cannot separate change from the disappearance of things, then what is called *infinite embodiment* must also be thought of in terms of *entropic embodiment*, as infinite change implies both creation and destruction. So the nothingness and meaninglessness of death cannot be avoided: every value is an embodied value that embodies its own infinity and death. But obviously this is not universally agreed upon. As stated earlier, there are many philosophers who reject the thesis that we should think of death in the negative terms of loss and nothingness. In this vein Irigaray argues that if we do not treat one another as possessions then there is no real loss.[11] The logic is quite simple: if we lay no claim to something then it cannot be taken from us. But since man doesn't typically follow this advice, he tends to perceive the world as a tumultuous abyss full of risk and peril.[12] Kelly Oliver draws from Irigaray's logic and terminology when she writes that the elements around us are full rather than empty, and because they are full we should not view them as threatening in the way that some traditional philosophers have imagined: "By forgetting air, the philosopher imagines that he is thrown into an empty abyss, where he confronts only nothingness. The abyss, [Irigaray] reminds us, is not empty; it is full of air. And air is not nothing."[13] The contrast here between fullness and emptiness is mirrored, then, by what sustains and nourishes us on one side and something violent, threatening, or tragic on the other. And this positive conception of reality is applied to death, as when Rosi Braidotti says of it that it is ultimately a generative, life-affirming force: "[Death is] the moment of ascetic dissolution of the subject; the moment of its merging with the web of non-human forces that frame him/her, the cosmos as a whole. We may call it death, but in a monistic ontology of vitalist materialism, it has rather to do with radical immanence."[14] Braidotti refers to radical immanence here because the individual life of the subject participates in an all-encompassing process of becoming in which nothing is fully lost or annihilated. This is why she interprets the death instinct, or the wish to die, as the "desire to live more intensely," because its ultimate goal is to merge with life on the holistic scale of the cosmos.[15] So death is hardly something to be feared: it is not emptiness, absence, and darkness, but a passageway to life forces greater than our own.

If we turn to the likes of Judith Butler and Jonathan Dollimore, however, the tone of the writing quickly changes. Butler thus describes the process of mourning as an acceptance of change that foils our best plans: "I think one is hit by waves and that one starts out the day with an aim, a project, a plan, and finds oneself foiled. One finds oneself fallen. One is exhausted but does not know why."[16] This process therefore acknowledges the loss as real and permanent. If there is no recuperation of it in the afterlife, or by way of merging with larger cosmic forces, then there is good reason for why we experience the grief that we do. By contrast, the so-called healthy approach in which life and death are seen as part of a natural continuum can be its own hypocritical form of denial as Dollimore puts forth: "This hope for a healthy attitude to death and loss is on occasions so trite it could itself be said to be blatantly symptomatic of the denial of death, being apparently incapable of acknowledging on the personal level just how devastating and unendurable death is or can be for those who survive."[17] I tend to agree with both of these authors: if there is something final and absolute about death, then the loss of someone close to us is bound to hurt on some level. And I don't think that this grief implies that we have treated that person as a possession, as if valuing or loving someone implies that they exist only for us. To the contrary, if we love someone we want that person to do well in life. We want that person to flourish as much as possible. So if we remain unaffected when a loved one suffers or dies, the appropriate term for this reaction is indifference. It is the antithesis of actually being invested in someone else's well-being.

But if it is responded that life and death are simply different aspects of a single cosmic life force in which every kind of loss is in truth nothing more than a process of merging with something larger than ourselves, then it is impossible to explain the origins and reality of grief that so many people do in fact experience. If the elements that sustain us are full rather than empty, so that death is itself a kind of generative life force, then the experience of anything at all, including that of change and death, should always be a positive, uplifting experience. The argument that our attachment to the individuated subject prevents us from seeing death as it truly is doesn't help here, for every moment of transition contained in the process of dying would be filled with greater and greater life-sustaining connections. Such a transition wouldn't be felt as a letting go of the self but as something much different—as the increasing reinforcement and strengthening of everything we love. But this is not always what we feel or experience, which says something meaningful about us. It says that we are mortal creatures who will from time to time undergo the kinds of loss that cannot be recuperated. And if we put any value at all in life, whether our own or that of others, then what we are affirming as good is the same thing that is permeated with the tragic nothingness of death.

We should keep this in mind as we return to the main themes of this chapter. If change is infinite and death absolute, then everything that we value should be referred to as entropic. In this sense there is no immortality drive, as Becker and others have posited, since the very condition of any drive is that it be connected to processes of temporality and dissolution. The same can be said of Foucault's concept of bio-power: if every investment of life is also an investment in the processes of change that are inherently self-destructive, then what is affirmed includes both life and death. It could be said that if we affirm life and death together it is only because we have no choice in the matter. If they weren't intimately bound up together as a single mortal phenomenon, then we would choose to live forever. There is some truth to this insofar as we do in fact pursue courses of action which help to solidify our own ways of life. If we value something then by definition, as stated previously, we want it to be present and available. And if we have another person in mind, such as a good friend, then we want that person to do well in life. But this line of thought only goes so far. We cannot value something that is absolute and never-changing, for the entire process of evaluation presupposes that we are satisfying particular needs and functions. That's why immortal life is a self-contradiction: it posits the continuation of desires and values in a world that entirely transcends all such limitations.

It follows, then, that when I say that I love this particular person, I do not have in mind someone who transcends space and time, but a person who is a unique being and therefore a member of the real world. The idea that, if possible, I would choose someone else to love if that other person were perfect in every way and therefore transcended all forms of finite embodiment doesn't make sense: this other person wouldn't be a person at all but mere nothingness. The only way in which we desire nothingness is in the shape and form of *entropic affirmation*, which means that we desire things in this world which are themselves permeated with change—the kind of change that ultimately destroys every particular form of reality. And while it is true that we do what we can to protect what we desire and love from being destroyed, it's not as if the process of change is only reluctantly affirmed: the things that we desire in this world are only found to be desirable insofar as they have identifiable traits and attributes, which is to say that an important part of what we find desirable about them is the fact that they are real, finite, and changing. But then it must be admitted that there is a certain paradox associated with this desire: on the one hand it is being said here that we of course do what we can to preserve the way of life that we value and desire, but on the other hand it is also being said that it is only possible to affirm that kind of life which is itself finite and mortal. This paradox, however, is a lived paradox. Insofar as life and death are always bound together, then this is simply how desire must be constituted. So this is much different from the contradiction stated above in reference to some kind of immortality drive, for in that case what is said to be desired, that is, life without conditions, cannot be lived at all.

The overarching argument, then, is that we cannot explain the scapegoating mechanism by way of an immortality drive. If the latter does not exist, then we need to give it up as a theoretical source for explaining anything at all. And there are many reasons for doubting its existence. The argument just provided above is one such reason: if the very condition of desire and its object is that both of them participate in the finite contours of embodiment, then the desire for life that transcends all such limits and parameters is a self-contradiction. Likewise, if change is infinite, then we cannot affirm anything apart from it. It's true that we are finite beings, but as such we are exposed to a perpetual movement of change that cannot be separated from whatever it is that we value. Another version of this argument is that the nothingness of death cannot be aligned more closely with some values rather than others. So while it's cliché to say that something like religious dogmatism can be explained as the repression of death (which is the flip side of the earlier arguments about an immortality drive), in truth all values do this equally. They do this because the emptiness and purposelessness of death is precisely that phenomenon which does away with all human measurements, so that no values can be said to be more open to it than others. And if we return to the other side of this argument concerning the maximization of life, then once again it has to be said that we can only measure differences in reference to particular goals and purposes.

This point can be clarified if we take an example in which it looks like one set of values is more life-maximizing than another, as in the comparison of an individual who sacrifices herself to save a stranger and someone else who thinks of nothing more highly than money, power, greed, etc. Now, even if it is true that the first person lived the kind of life in which she never scapegoated others, my contention is that this would have had nothing to do with a greater or lesser form of bio-power (or the maximization of life). And the reason why we cannot make distinctions on this basis, at least in a general way, is because the maximization of anything can only be measured in terms of something specific. If there is no predetermined goal to life, then neither is there is a predetermined form of its maximization. So the woman who sacrifices herself lived the kind of life that maximized one set of goals, while the person who pursued the path of money maximized another. And in both cases there were infinite variations of life that were not maximized at all. Finally, if it's said that transitioning away from the general aspects of the scapegoating mechanism need not require much of a change in its overall logic, I would disagree. If Terry Eagleton is wrong to claim, for example, that there is a connection between the "disavowal of death" or the "immortality of the will" and various military aggressions, then the problem to be critiqued will have much less to do with the idea that we are willing too much than with a particular variable or factor in that process.[18]

It should be acknowledged, however, that in a certain sense every author considered above does in fact analyze scapegoating in reference to specific facts, details, and concerns. Richard Kearney, for instance, argues that we should be wary of the concept of infinite responsibility when it fails to distinguish between "benign and malign others."[19] As there is no responsibility to remain open to the individual or group whose intention is to harm us, we must develop the capacity to discern when this is the case. And often times when we fail to do so it is because we are guilty of scapegoating. So if we wish to become more discerning in our relations with others, it is imperative that we overcome this tendency. This seems exactly right to me, except that Kearney's analysis defines such a tendency in relation to an alterity that resides deep within us.[20] So while it is true that Kearney remains attentive to the particular aspects of alterity that take place in our exchanges with others, he nonetheless repeats the familiar argument that openness to something uncanny or uncontainable is what will help us to fight back against scapegoating: "The self-other relation . . . reveals a practice of ethical 'conscience' which is the other inscribed within me as an uncontainable call from *beyond*. . . . Here the very ipseity of the self expresses itself, paradoxically and marvellously, as openness to otherness. Real hospitality."[21] It is certainly true, then, that the self-other relation is for Kearney defined by its narrative and hermeneutical qualities, but we are nevertheless expected to remain open to an uncontainable call that teaches us to be more peaceful, understanding, and hospitable. The arguments I have marshalled forth above, however, make it doubtful that we can end scapegoating on this basis. If there is truly something infinite, incommensurable, or uncontainable within each of us, then it becomes impossible to know which values are more open to it than others. It also becomes impossible to say which ones are more totalizing, as this is just another way of distinguishing openness from closure.[22] And if this distinction cannot be made, then the argument put forth by Kearney, Eagleton, Spivak, and others claiming that we can bring more people together by critiquing our totalizing, transcendental sets of values should be rejected.[23] Furthermore, once we do this, we will find to our surprise that the equation of scapegoating with a projection of death and otherness is itself a fundamental scapegoating mistake.

If the previous statement seems paradoxical it is because we have equated the creation of social divisions via the projection of alterity with the essence of scapegoating for such a long time. We therefore read in Girard's analysis that "the principle of mimetic desire, its rivalries, and the internal divisions it creates are identical with the equally mimetic principle that unifies society: the scapegoat."[24] It should be noticed here that the creation of internal rifts and divisions is not only linked to the basic scapegoating mechanism but actually identified with it.[25] But if this is a false identification, then there will be many cases in which a projection leads to a social division without that having anything to do with scapegoating. It may be, in other words, that many of these cases are the inevitable result of what it means to affirm life and death simultaneously in all values. As argued above, if the drive to immortality doesn't exist, then the desire to either expand or solidify our values can only go so far. We do not want, that is to say, for them to be entirely integrated with the social world around them. In this way, the affirmation of values that have a self-destructive aspect is an important part of the explanation for why there will always be rivalries and divisions: it proves that we do not want all other values and ways of life to support the existence of our own. In this sense *entropic affirmation*, which is the affirmation of death and nothingness, necessarily leads to *entropic refraction*, which is the projection or displacement of that nothingness onto the larger social field by way of divisions.

In response it could be said that even if displacement is necessary it need not manifest itself through social divisions and agonistic relationships. Instead we might embrace the inherent tragedies of life and death more evenly, so that the ideal goal would be to achieve some kind of equilibrium across as many social groups as possible. This concept of equilibrium, though, takes up a purely defensive stance toward death and otherness. Similar to Foucault's notion of security, it would minimize risks and disruptions as much as possible. It refuses to admit that all values necessarily give rise to points of dissolution in the social field. By contrast, the argument from entropic affirmation has put forth that the death instinct is real and that we cannot desire anything without also desiring its inevitable destruction, suggesting that even when we actively and directly seek to expand our values we also desire, perhaps indirectly, that there be points of separation and counter-resistance on the part of others. So the idea that our own values actively contribute to the breaking apart of the social field, as opposed to this only happening passively, defensively, or begrudgingly, is what seems to be most consistent with entropic affirmation. The idea that we can avoid scapegoating by creating values that do not lend themselves to some kind of social division is therefore a false one.[26] There will always be entropic refraction. It follows, then, that Girard's identification of scapegoating with every form of rivalry is itself a primary manifestation of scapegoating as it denies and projects the refraction which is unavoidable in each of us.

To summarize, if we affirm any values at all they must be the sort of values that are simultaneously expansive and self-destructive. Even as we seek to connect them harmoniously with the world around us, by way of economics, socialization, technology, and so forth, there is a limit to this since we do not want to live forever. If we did, we would pursue the path of bio-power and strengthen as many social relations as possible with as many social groups as possible. But since we do not, the process of entropic refraction follows from that of entropic affirmation insofar as our values necessitate some kind of resistance and pushback from within the larger social field. If the goal of equilibrium were something that we actually pursued, it would imply that we do not want for there to be any such divisions among values. It would mean that all of our interactions with others, across all cultures, could be motivated by a simple desire to make as many life-enhancing connections as possible. However, if the death instinct cannot be so easily removed from those values, then such a desire does not exist. And that is exactly what entropic affirmation entails, namely, that we ourselves introduce the death instinct into the larger social context whenever we affirm any values at all. Furthermore, as it is the nature and reality of death that it tears us away from the world in which we live, it follows that what it introduces into our social reality would have a similar effect, namely, contributing to points of separation and division. And if this is true, then it follows that scapegoating mustn't be identified with *all* such divisions, but only with those that are avoidable and unnecessary. To put an end to scapegoating, then, requires being able to find the most likely source of a problem or crisis. When we falsely attribute this to an outside social group, we are creating a division that is not only avoidable but distracts us from addressing the real problem. But when we argue that *all* forms of division should be overcome, then we ourselves become more likely to project and attribute what we don't like about ourselves onto others. So when it is said that only certain types of values—typically those that are connected to bio-power, the simulacrum, an immortality drive, instrumental rationality, and so forth—are the ones that lend themselves to the creation of social divisions via the projection of finitude and death, what is actually being denied on behalf of some values while being identified with others is the fact that all of them have this tendency. And it is only when this tendency mistakes, purposely or not, one source of a problem for another that we should begin to think about it in terms of scapegoating.

By contrast, Matthias Fritsch argues against the necessity of antagonistic divisions when they are derived from the theoretical resources of deconstruction. He therefore rejects the notion, as defended by Chantal Mouffe and Ernesto Laclau, that the constitutive outside associated with every form of identity must be (1) clearly demarcated from the inside, (2) identified with concrete humans, and (3) necessarily antagonistic.[27] Although these are brilliant objections, I do not think they apply to what has been argued thus far in this chapter. For example, I do agree that the limits between the inside and the outside, or one social group and another, are permeable, fluctuating, and contingent. But this in itself doesn't imply that the limits, while they last, don't have meaning for us. We cannot help but to impose form on the world via different kinds of social values, and thus we delimit ourselves accordingly—even if such a delimitation is imperfect and subject to change. The term that best captures this reality is therefore *agonistic pathos*, as it implies that we share something profound even with those who contest and possibly undermine our values. Perhaps, however, the agonistic relation need not refer to other humans. Fritsch thus writes that what is excluded from our own particular social field need not be another social group but instead something nonhuman, as with an "imaginary value, a phantasm, or the gods, animals, and so forth."[28] Becker, in a similar vein, argued that if there must be a relation of antagonism it should be redirected away from other humans toward more impersonal objects like natural disasters.[29] The answer to this objection was intimated when discussing the goal of social equilibrium: on the assumption that entropic affirmation is real and valid, we do not simply take up a defensive posture toward all threats, natural or otherwise, but through refraction create divisions within the social field that put our own values at risk. And since we are the ones creating these values, the divisions that arise as a result of this process have to do with real, living human beings, not imaginary gods or entities. Nevertheless, even if it is acknowledged that our values always include an exclusionary aspect in relation to other social groups, it doesn't follow from this alone that such a relation must be agonistic, competitive, or adversarial. It may be, as Fritsch continues with his final objection, that a "friend-friend relation" is sufficient for establishing identity in relationship to an outside or other.[30] As there's no reason to assume that friendships must be totalizing, they could satisfy the deconstructive idea that the same and the other are never fully integrated while undermining Mouffe's claim that this implies some kind of necessary antagonism. But this returns us once again to the issue of an equilibrium: if it were true that we only ever desire what is positive and life-enhancing, then we would do whatever we could to replace every harm with mutually beneficial relationships. But since this is *not* the case, it does seem that we affirm, sometimes unconsciously and indirectly, the existence of values that contest, counter, and undermine our own. So it would be a mistake to think that we can or should eradicate the agonistic aspect from all social relationships. Nevertheless, it can be sublimated. What is agonistic in one domain, as with military conflicts, can be channeled into another, as with economics and culture. What this means for the overall agonistic orientation of our values will therefore now be considered.

NOTES

1. Becker, *Escape from Evil*.
2. Oliver, *Witnessing: Beyond Recognition*.
3. Becker, *Escape from Evil*, 109.
4. Richard Kearney, *Strangers, Gods, and Monsters: Interpreting Otherness* (London and New York: Routledge, 2003), 26.
5. Ibid., 77.
6. But this doesn't overturn what was said above about equal embodiment and affirmation. Since infinite change both passes through and surpasses us, there is nothing illogical about including and excluding it at the same time.

7. One reason given for this equality had to do with the impossibility of measuring the infinite aspect of change that is embodied in our values even as it transcends them. If this way of framing it seems to rely too heavily on a quantitative assessment, it can be restated in terms of meaning or value: as there is no internal moral standard that guides the ongoing changes of the universe or inhabits the nothingness of death, then it is false to argue, once again, that some values are more closely aligned to these processes and events than others.

8. Simon Critchley, *Infinitely Demanding: Ethics of Commitment, Politics of Resistance* (London and New York: Verso, 2007), 21.

9. Badiou, *Ethics: An Essay on the Understanding of Evil*, 12; Badiou, *L'éthique: essai sur la conscience du mal*, 14.

10. It's true that I believe that the infinite affects the orientation and structure of our values, but this is different from arguing that what is ethically proper is to remain open to some kind of infinite demand. In the latter case we cannot stipulate how it is possible to distinguish varying degrees of openness, responsiveness, or denial.

11. Irigaray, *To Be Two*, 43.

12. Ibid., 69.

13. Oliver, *Witnessing: Beyond Recognition*, 213.

14. Braidotti, *The Posthuman,* 136.

15. Ibid., 134.

16. Butler, *Precarious Life: The Powers of Mourning and Violence*, 21.

17. Jonathan Dollimore, *Death, Desire, and Loss in Western Culture* (New York: Routledge, 1998), 123.

18. Eagleton, *After Theory*, 187.

19. Kearney, *Strangers, Gods, and Monsters*, 67.

20. Ibid., 5.

21. Ibid., 81.

22. While I do not think that we can make this distinction vis-à-vis something infinite or uncontainable, there is no reason why we can't do so in the context of specific values. So when we embrace one way of life as opposed to another, it follows that we have excluded all sorts of values to varying degrees—and thus in reference to these values we might say that we have totalized our own. But in this sense of totalization there is nothing inherently wrong, as we may have good reason for excluding *specific* forms of values, alterity, and otherness.

23. Gayatri Chakravorty Spivak, *Nationalism and the Imagination* (London and New York: Seagull Books, 2010), 42, 54, and 68–71.

24. René Girard, *The Scapegoat*, trans. Yvonne Freccero (Baltimore: Johns Hopkins University Press, 1986), 187; René Girard, *Le bouc émissaire* (Paris: B. Grasset, 1982), 263.

25. This is a critical difference. Although I am denying here that the creation of social divisions by way of projection and displacement should be equated with scapegoating, that's not to say that it can't or shouldn't be a crucial part of the explanation—as we shall see.

26. Indeed, what is the creation of a division in the social field but an instance of dissolution? So the argument here in its simplest form is that the affirmation of death

is also the affirmation of divisions: we do not desire that our values have only strong, life-preserving connections with all other values in the world. Of course there will be many instances in which the introduction of a social division is intended to lead to greater power and strength, much as the breakdown of muscles can lead to their growth, but the principle of entropic refraction rejects this from always being the case.

27. Matthias Fritsch, "Antagonism and Democratic Citizenship (Schmitt, Mouffe, Derrida)," *Research in Phenomenology* 38, no. 2 (2008): 181.

28. Ibid., 184.

29. Becker, *Escape from Evil*, 144–45.

30. Fritsch, "Antagonism and Democratic Citizenship," 185.

Chapter 6

Dolls and Death

If there is something infinitely mysterious about death, then it must be difficult to say what it is exactly that makes it so mysterious. In a certain sense its meaning transcends us, in the sense that it seems to challenge all human constructions of meaning. Whatever we believe, and whatever we embrace, seems to vanish into nothingness as soon as it is touched by the purposelessness of death. What is perhaps most strange about this mystery of nothingness, which is itself the inevitable culmination of a world in flux, is the fact that we are so familiar with it. It is both inside of us and all around us. It is in the news and the movies, but it is also buried deep within us. Krzysztof Michalski says it perfectly: "Death—in its absurdity, its incomprehensibility, its mystery—permeates my life, is hidden in everything I know in living. The meaning of my life . . . cannot be understood without this other, dark side, without this nonsense, this incommensurability, this transcendence."[1] This is a powerful insight, implying that what is absurd and incommensurable carries over into all aspects of life. There is no hiding from this fundamental fact. There is no escape to safety. There is only absurdity underlying everything that we do and believe. If we imagine that this isn't the case, that such incomprehensibility is merely provisional, then it would have to be shown that death is an illusion, or some kind of passageway to a more meaningful world. Of course, we are familiar with how this might be done. It can be said that whatever we believe about death is nothing more than a projection of insecurities, anxieties, and fears. And this in turn can be explained by reference to the attachments of the ego, so that if we give up such attachments we will simultaneously give up the illusions of the ego and everything associated with it—including its death. It can also be said, from another perspective, that the human self is animated by an immortal soul that will survive the mortality of the physical body. If a persuasive argument could be made on behalf of such claims, then death would be less than an infinite mystery. It would be something knowable and comprehensible. Far from posing an intractable problem for us, death would be susceptible to human control and mastery, whether through science, art, religion, spirituality, technological advances, or anything else that can be dreamed up. These are issues and questions pertaining to sublimation, because what we want to know is whether or not the loss associated with death is something that can be recuperated. If this is indeed possible, then the work of sublimation would be one of transforming the sense of loss into an overall positive experience. But if it is not, then we need to reconsider the limits of transformative recuperation.

One way of defending the claim that death is an illusion is based on the metaphysical assumption that all things are one.[2] If this were true, then any form of individuation would likewise be an illusion, including the self and all of its thoughts and perceptions. This is in fact a fundamental and familiar premise in the teachings of Buddhism: "The instructed disciple of the Noble Ones does not regard material shape as self, or self as having material shape, or material shape as being in the self, or the self as being in material shape. Nor does he regard feeling, perception, the impulses, or consciousness in any of these ways."[3] Anything that has form and shape, then, is an illusion. And the reason that anything of this nature is not real is precisely because of its ephemeral condition. Hence the disciple "comprehends each of these aggregates as it really is, that it is impermanent, suffering, not-self, compounded, woeful."[4] We should therefore release ourselves from all bounded reality, and if we do this we will no longer experience pain, incompletion, or *dukkha*. It is only when we attach ourselves to things that have limits, to things that are perceived in space and time, that we experience disappointment. But if we extinguish our cravings and appetites then we will instead be at peace with ourselves, for then we will have replaced impermanent objects of desire with pure emptiness and nirvana. There is, however, a paradox associated with this kind of experience that transcends all individual boundaries. If what we have in mind is something that takes place in the world of change observed all around us, then the impermanence of that change will still affect the experience that is said to be pure emptiness. But if it is replied that the experience takes place apart from such changing circumstances, then it would be separated from a specific form of reality, which is to say that it would be defined by the kind of limitation that it was intended to overcome. So either it takes place in a world of fluctuation, which undercuts its status as unchanging, or it paradoxically creates a new kind of limit by attempting to overcome everything associated with limits and conditions. Perhaps it will then be said that change is pure illusion, something fabricated on the basis of false attachments. If that were the case, then the experience of nothingness would in fact be completely harmonious with the world which we experience as changing—as the latter would be nothing more than a false perception. But that's not a very promising view to take, as it is plagued by the very old problem of trying to explain how the illusion of change *arises* from a situation of pure oneness and stillness. So in this way we cannot avoid the observation that in a world without change not even the illusion of change can arise as that would assume, by definition, some kind of change.

It thus seems preferable to agree that change is an illusion in the sense that it is impermanent,[5] but not in the sense that it doesn't take place at all. All things come to an end, and thus they participate in a form of virtual existence. But what comes to an end only does so because it undergoes an incessant movement of change and self-destruction. If, to the contrary, it were to survive this process of changing appearances and circumstances, it would have to be immortal. So while Buddhism teaches us that there is no permanent self, the argument here would be exactly the opposite: in the physical world all things change except for that part of human existence which has been granted to us by the divine creator. By focusing on this part, the spiritual part, there is hope of transcending the tragedies and tribulations associated with temporal matter. But despite the different approach in terms of metaphysical assumptions, the problem here is very much the same as the one above: if it is true that that there is something impervious to change, whether it is said to be pure nothingness or pure spirit, it becomes difficult to imagine how it coexists with the actual world in which we live. If this world is one of change, then it seems that any interaction taking place in it will participate in its impermanence. To say that there is a kind of reality that will always remain exactly what it is, absolutely one with itself at all times, is to describe something that has *no* interaction with the fleeting circumstances of our actual world. And if there is no interaction between the immortal soul within us and the physical world of our embodiment, then we cannot explain how so many of us confuse one for the other. We cannot explain, in other words, all of those cases in which we identify ourselves with something physical—as with our physical bodies. If we assume that the real self is kept together by something eternal and unchanging, then it is not the sort of thing that should lose sight of its own identity. That would presuppose a change from one state to another, from perfect self-identity to being confused with something which it is not. And such a change is incompatible with the pure stasis of an eternal being. The natural conclusion, then, is that we are indeed finite, changing, embodied creatures for whom death is absolutely final.

This in itself is not an original observation, but is one that needs to be further explored if we hope to understand the limits and possibilities of sublimation. To that end, what must be noticed first of all is that the embodiment of life includes its own absence and invisibility. If life is embodied rather than eternal, if it never comes to a standstill, then it undergoes the kind of change that carries the absence of death within itself. And as Derrida puts forth in *Specters of Marx*, the unity (without synthesis) of what we see with what we do not has more in common with ghosts rather than spirits: "This transcendence is not altogether spiritual, it retains that bodiless body which we have recognized as making the difference between specter and spirit. What surpasses the senses still passes before us in the silhouette of the sensuous body that it nevertheless lacks or that remains inaccessible to us."[6] The invisibility of life is in this way both immanent and transcendent. If it were entirely the latter, then it would be pure spirit, which is to say, pure, absolute, complete life. It would be entirely free of the body. The specter, by contrast, is what Derrida refers to as the bodiless body, as it is the body that is both here and not here, both present and absent. It is true that the immediate context of the above quote pertains to the life of the commodity, but as one might expect Derrida makes the same case for use-value: there are no absolute distinctions here between processes of life that are haunted and those that are not.[7] As soon as it is agreed that life is mortal, that it is full of change and self-destruction, then it must also be agreed that what we see in it can never be fully seen or identified: it always transcends us even as it "passes before us."

Earlier it was stated that all things participate in a form of virtual existence which is simultaneously real as well as unreal. This seems especially relevant to the above argument pertaining to the embodiment of life: if it were true that there were something immortal within us, something that could not be hindered by the spatial and temporal limitations of human embodiment, then it would follow that everything in the universe would sustain our existence. There would be nothing opposed to us, as that would by definition constitute a threat to the concept that we were indeed immortal creatures.[8] But since we know that this is not the case, that in fact we will one day die, it follows that our place in the world is fragile, vulnerable, and even unreal. In this case, then, what is meant by the unreal is that we are not firmly connected to a reality that sustains us in every possible way. We are incomplete and dispossessed. But at the same time there is *also* something real about us. We are not self-enclosed individuals without any connection whatsoever to reality. To say that we are embodied creatures is to say the opposite. It is to say that we are vulnerable to the conditions of space and time that operate everywhere. So while it is not possible to attain full connectedness with the world around us, as if we enjoyed a firm place in it, it doesn't follow that there aren't any connections at all. They are ephemeral, but they are still connections. In this way, what is meant by virtual existence or virtual embodiment, as we shall see in our discussion of Hans Bellmer's photos, drawings, and writings, is that we exist in the world without doing so completely. We are connected to the world, that is to say, even as we are slipping away from it.

This line of thought applies to everything embodied, including all of our thoughts, feelings, and perceptions. All of them are therefore virtual in the sense that they are both real and unreal. But it is very important to keep in mind the semantics of these words. Although we can describe these processes as either virtual or illusory in the way that I have done thus far, it is sometimes more convenient, at least for purposes of clarity, to maintain a conceptual distinction between what is virtual and what is real. The former would therefore apply to what is transient and disconnected while the latter would remind us that the only things that disappear are things that exist in some fashion or another. And as long as we are nonidentical beings, changing from moment to moment, there is no way around this predicament: we exist in the world without any recourse to something in itself beyond the virtual. If it were the opposite, if we were the sorts of beings with a self-identical essence or an immortal soul, then we could separate what is real in itself from what is fake and unreal. We could ground ourselves and all of our thoughts in what is absolutely valid and unchanging. And since we ourselves would no longer undergo change, our thoughts and perceptions of the world would likewise remain eternally fixed. What we now take to be the inside of the subject would be perfectly aligned with the truths of the outside world. In fact, there would no longer be any borders between the inside and the outside, as that would imply a limitation on the power of the subject, thereby threatening its claim to eternal self-identity. In this thought experiment there would be no actual embodiment of the subject. There would only be full and absolute presence, which is to say, the seamless unity of the subject not only with itself but everything else as well.

Assuming this is not the case, Derrida is right to describe language as supplemental, as a series of substitutions in which we connect with the world even as it escapes us. Accordingly, there is nothing in this world which can be perceived, thought about, or enjoyed without it simultaneously resisting us: "The enjoyment of the *thing itself* is thus undermined, in its act and in its essence, by frustration. One cannot therefore say that it has an essence or an act (*eidos, ousia, energeia*, etc.). Something promises itself as it escapes, gives itself as it moves away, and strictly speaking it cannot even be called presence."[9] So it is that every time we reach out to something outside of ourselves, to things in the world, we do so in a way that ensures that we never firmly grasp anything at all. If every moment is a moment of change, then our connections with the outside can only take place if those connections are already contaminated by such change, which would imply some kind of perpetual substitution. Hence, in this way, we never gain access to a pure referent outside of all substitutions and supplements: every mode of expression is automatically displaced from itself as well any other point of reference. But it doesn't follow from this that the outside is entirely linguistic, social, or

subjective. It would be incorrect to infer from our lack of a transcendental signified, or a pure thing in itself, that the outside is nothing more than a function
of the inside. If it is right that the temporality of experience necessitates ongoing displacements, then sharp divisions between the inside and the outside
are unrealistic. These supplemental displacements ensure that the inside does
not coincide with itself, therefore it cannot be clearly demarcated from what
it is not: the other, the outside, the abyss, heterogeneity, and so on. So when
Derrida writes that "there is nothing outside of the text,"[10] the reasonable
interpretation is that we only gain access to the outside by way of those same
displacements that make experience and language possible. So while they
make the latter possible, it is by no means the case that they make either
of them all-powerful or ubiquitous. As Derrida himself has remarked about
the above quote, his intention was quite the opposite. Contrary to several
misinterpretations, it was a matter of putting into question "the authority of
linguistics," so that the notion of a text was "introduced to mark the limits of
the linguistic turn."[11]

These limits would not exist, according to Derrida, if it weren't for the
inevitability of death. It is the latter condition that guarantees a finite perspective, one which will never have complete control over its own desire.[12]
It may be that we desire for the inside and the outside, or the subject and
the world, to be unified in an experience of presence, but this desire, being
finite, guarantees its own failure.[13] In this way the supplement is not only
a substitute for what we desire and try to understand, but it is at the same
time a substitute for death and emptiness. If we were complete in ourselves,
there would be no reason to pursue anything at all. Desire would not exist.
The movement of desire therefore operates by way of supplements which
help us to connect with the world but also embody the absence without
which there would be no desire in the first place. With the necessary caveats,
this is comparable to Freud's compulsion to repeat, in which a primordial
instinct overrides the desire for pleasure and happiness. In both cases we
observe different aspects of our being, one focused on life and the other on
death, intimately bound up together so that one aspect or drive cannot be
separated from the other. Of course, it is possible to read the compulsion to
repeat as a normalizing defense against trauma, as an understandable way to
prevent something horrific from happening again. On this model, dreams that
reenact a previous traumatic event ultimately serve the pleasure principle, if
somewhat belatedly, through their dedication to the unity and survival of the
subject. Hal Foster is right, however, to point out the irrational dimension.
When desire and loss are bound together via compulsion, it is not always possible to distinguish which aspect of our being is serving the other. Keeping in
mind Freud's description of instinctual life in terms of how we are compelled
to restore a primordial form of existence, Foster asks the incisive question,

"If all drives are ultimately conservative, can that of life finally be opposed to that of death?"[14] At this point his answer should be clear: if desire and pleasure are themselves the embodiment of change, then even though they do what they can to sustain their existence, they are not for that reason any less self-destructive.

The main explanation for this can be traced back to one of the fundamental premises of Derrida's deconstruction, namely, that nothing is simple.[15] There are no discrete elements, in language or outside of language. Hence, everything is both itself and what it is not—albeit without synthesis. Everything is the thing that it is and the absence of the thing that it is. And although this signifies a certain finitude on our part, in terms of our inherent limitations, it also reminds us that our finitude takes place in relationship to infinite change—both within ourselves and all around us. As said many times before, we would be self-enclosed entities if we weren't undergoing the kind of change that makes us nonidentical. So this change makes us finite, but it thereby places us in a context in which we are related to the nothingness of death as well as the infinity of a universe that doesn't stand still. In the former case, the absence of an entity or individual can be described as infinite in the sense that it transcends all finite modes of intelligence and comprehension. Only things that exist have limits, and thus by definition that which ceases to exist is no longer constrained by the boundaries of finite existence. Earlier it was remarked that we cannot embody either pure nothingness or pure life, as every form of embodiment imposes limits on such purity. Now it may seem that this principle has been contradicted, but that is not the case: although the finitude of life is related to its pure absence and nothingness, it does not embody this nothingness within itself without change making it what it is not, that is, the same, the self, and the limited. So what was previously rejected wasn't so much the embodiment of nothingness as its embodiment *without embodiment*. And in the latter case pertaining to the infinite change that is everywhere around us, Derrida writes that the textuality of the text presupposes an abyss, "an indefinitely multiplied structure," that moves beyond presence even as it opens it up to its own exorbitance.[16] This relation of the embodiment of the text (or the self) to an infinite abyss may seem like an unfounded, unsubstantiated presupposition. But it has been argued above on several occasions that nonidentity cannot be secured by fixed boundaries. So it is in this way, I take it, that the experience of presence as absence, or vice versa, has immediate implications for the kind of world which makes this nonidentity possible. And it is not a world in which everything has its identifiable place within fixed parameters, but exactly the opposite: it is an abyss of change in all directions which facilitates the loss of things and loved ones without any hope for return.

It goes without saying, or at least it should, that we desire some coherence in our lives. The world is intrinsically meaningless, but that doesn't imply that we wander about it aimlessly. Indeed, the fact that we desire or need anything at all indicates that our relationship to the world is at least somewhat rational, pragmatic, and functional. But if the world, despite temporary patterns of coherence, is likewise an abyss of change that guarantees our nonidentical condition, then every new embodiment of a satisfied desire will necessarily repeat the existential conflicts (between presence and absence, identity and nonidentity, interiority and exteriority) that take place at every level of growth and development. That's not to say that they are always lived in the same way, as that would ignore social and historical variations, but at no point do we overcome our finitude and all of the paradoxes that go with it. We are therefore immersed in these paradoxes, and everything that we do and say reinterprets them in a new form of embodiment. It might even be said that there is something automatic about this kind of repetition. In the opening lines of the *Little Anatomy of the Physical Unconscious, or The Anatomy of the Image*, the artist Hans Bellmer explicitly affirms this possibility. He thus writes that every kind of expression—from words and sounds to actions and gestures—is the result of a single "law of birth," namely, the reflex.[17] For Bellmer, this reflex proceeds by way of something painful or prohibited, as with his first example of a toothache. So if in response to a toothache, or any other source of pain and excitation, my left hand contracts into the form of a fist, the reflex here is one of transforming the original pain into an artificial or virtual point of reference. What is important here in terms of nonidentity, as with the nonidentity of pain,[18] is that what is considered to be real or original is perpetually divided against itself in the formation of new focal points. These focal points cannot be created, that is to say, without taking the original source of pain and projecting it away from itself, thereby fragmenting the self into different areas of focus, both real and virtual.

In every bodily expression, then, there is a projection of something that is missing or absent. If we refer back to the image of a clenched fist, for example, we do not readily observe in it the projection of a toothache, even though each body part is said to be fused in this way. The reason for this is that the real and the virtual do not entirely coincide. In place of this projected unity, an "iridescent gap" keeps them from converging.[19] In this manner, according to Bellmer, we are dominated by an irrational and absurd tendency to assert the individual reality of the self through means which are opposed to that reality. It is the "impossible itself," he writes, that is thereby realized.[20] So there is no form of embodiment that is capable of transcending this back-and-forth logic of projection and nonidentity: every time we overcome one set of oppositions we necessarily and automatically embody another. But that's not to say, for Bellmer at least, that there aren't deeper forms of reconciliation. So when he asserts, perhaps with Freud in mind, that the main instinct of life is "to escape from the contours of the self," what is at stake is a primordial reconciliation of ourselves with the world (and everything that is outside of the ego).[21] The primary aim of the reflex, then, is to overcome all boundaries and divisions. But this cannot be achieved as long as we are attached to the self, which is by definition finite and limited. Bellmer's statements against reason and utility can therefore be understood in this light, insofar as they tend to serve the impossible task of making the individual one with itself. Such a task is necessarily impossible since the finite individual, undergoing continual change, will one day die. But what is impossible on the limited scale of the self is not so on the larger scale of nature and all of its perpetual transformations. There is a deeper, universal principle at work on this larger scale in which the individual is reconciled with everything that otherwise seems hostile, threatening, or other.[22] From these sorts of observations Bellmer concludes on a therapeutic note: "It is at these times of 'solution' that a fear shorn of terror can be transformed into a feeling of living at a heightened power; to appear to be one—even beyond birth and death—with the tree, the 'other,' and fate's necessary strokes of chance, to remain almost 'oneself' on the other side."[23]

Although there are good reasons to remain skeptical of this universal principle, its consideration forces us to think through an interesting paradox in Bellmer. On the one hand, he writes that we want nothing more than to escape the confines of the self. Assuming that the self represents life, the natural inference would be that this desire is a manifestation of the death drive. On the other hand, he also puts forth that every response to pain creates new focal points within and around the self, thereby prolonging life through new forms of embodiment. Moreover, throughout Bellmer's work these different forms of embodiment are associated with a variety of artificial representations, thus bringing to mind a defensive attitude toward death. This is most obvious when his dolls are either composed of or surrounded by walls. In Sue Taylor's analysis these walls, oftentimes depicted as female figures, represent a desire to return to the womb: "The brick wall and the dove in Bellmer's work are icons of disavowal or denial. With the wall, the artist literalizes and externalizes his defensive response to shock. This protective strategy is not unrelated to his fantasies of returning to the safety of the womb."[24] This interpretation is confirmed by Bellmer himself when he writes of a deeper unity with nature beyond death (assuming that such unity is one more form of denial). And the fact that the dolls with which he identifies are often placed within womb-like structures, as we see in the 1934 drawings *Interior of the Brick Doll* and *Peppermint Tower IV*, provides us with visual corroboration. But the metaphor of the womb is a complicated and ambiguous one. Therese Lichtenstein's description of it in Bellmer's work is less reassuring: "The image of the womb as a place of enclosure exists in Bellmer's physically and psychologically claustrophobic photographs of the doll. The doll appears buried in tomblike enclosures."[25] She also adds that when we see an image of the artist depicted in this way, as we do in *Double Cephalopod (Self-Portrait with Unica Zürn)* (1955), what we see is Bellmer's disembodied head in the body of his lover. So the womb can be associated not only with life and safety but also with death, decapitation, and dismemberment. And this interpretation, no less than Taylor's, is in keeping with Bellmer's comments on displaced nonidentity: if it is true that every focal point of life-affirmation is virtual in some way, then the depiction of the body as layered with either bricks or plastic reminds us that the contours of our existence are never entirely real or stable.

The experience of the double has the same effect. There are many intimations of it throughout Bellmer's work, as with the images of twin dolls or multiple body parts extended from a single source, but there is one in particular that is easy to overlook. It is an untitled 1934 drawing of a hand holding a glass marble. The first clue that this image of the hand may be related to an experience of the double (as a projection of the viewer) is the marble itself. As with the ball joint or protuberant belly, the marble is associated with magical qualities in the sense that every focal point gives rise to some set of "substitutions or virtualities."[26] If the focal point is an experience of nonidentity, as with the toothache discussed earlier, then the substitutions embody the transference of that experience elsewhere, as with other body parts and outside objects. In the image of the hand holding the marble, then, what we see before us is one more kind of substitution. In this case, however, the virtual projection (or double) is of ourselves. In this way it seems that we are observing one of our own hands turned back toward us, thereby displacing our experience of ourselves as fully stable or unified. And this process of fragmentation follows the same logic explained above that the virtual focal point, in this case the image of a hand, is created through a process of self-division. This is a fair assumption given that the viewer doesn't fully identify with what she sees, as it is a piece of artwork, implying that such an identification takes place only on the condition that the viewer experiences the image as both inside and outside of her self-identity. Perhaps the best way to describe this experience, then, is in terms of the uncanny. It reminds us that we are not fully here or there, but that instead we exist both inside *and* outside of ourselves. If we are not exactly one with ourselves, in other words, then the affirmation of the self takes place through projections which are both real and not real. And if they are not entirely real, then they do not merely embody new forms of the subject but also inevitably undermine it. If this is right, then this is one more reiteration of the paradox that in these (often sadomasochistic) images life is affirmed through self-destructive processes.

The double therefore always has more than one meaning: "These ideas [of doubling] arose on the soil of boundless self-love . . . and when this phase is surmounted, the meaning of the 'double' changes: having once been an assurance of immortality, it becomes the uncanny harbinger of death."[27]

In this discussion of ambiguity between the inside and the outside, or the real and the virtual, one argument is that more attentiveness to it is needed in the critique of unjust power mechanisms. Hal Foster writes in this vein when he suggests that Bellmer's images of corpselike, fragmented dolls contested the purified ideals of the body that were portrayed in Nazi art during that time.[28] Therese Lichtenstein adds that the doll images inverted fascist paradigms of sex and race that projected impurity onto social groups whose persecution was thereby justified: "The type of physical and psychological deviance that the doll exhibits is precisely the form of 'degeneracy' associated by the Nazis with Jews, socialists, blacks, gay men and lesbians, modern artists, and the insane."[29] It is by investing in such paradigms of the purified body that we are all the more likely to project what we despise about ourselves onto others. If we cannot accept the fact that life is the embodiment of death, that every desire is conditioned by finitude, then we need an explanation for the origins of pain, suffering, and tragedy. One such explanation is that our group is on the path to eternal life, whereas other groups are not. In this way it is the other groups who are to blame for the miserable, tragic conditions of life throughout the world. The unfortunate irony is that this strategy perpetuates and worsens those conditions which it otherwise seeks to overcome. Assuming that each of us is finite, as we should, then the argument of Foster, Lichtenstein, and others is that the above strategy is an impossible one: there is no purified realm of life that exists on its own, apart from this world. And if this strategy is untenable, then a new one is needed—one which accepts the fragility and finitude of life's contours. This in itself doesn't guarantee less tragedy or injustice, but it does lay down the necessary groundwork. Derrida thus associates hospitality with finitude and inhospitality with the presence of full life: "Present existence or essence has never been the condition, object, or the thing of justice. . . . One must constantly remember that this absolute evil (which is, is it not, absolute life, fully present life, the one that does not know death and does not want to hear about it) can take place."[30] Derrida, perhaps somewhat surprisingly, is being quite clear: if we wish to mitigate injustice, then we must first move away from the idea of life as full and present and instead accept it as incomplete and self-differentiating.

In this book I have argued in a number of different ways against such a distinction between greater and lesser openness to finitude. The concept of entropic affirmation stipulates that all values affirm death equally, without any degrees of difference. As long as death is a phenomenon that leads to the absence of embodiment and meaning, then we have no basis for saying which of our values are more in line with it than others. That which is formless cannot be said to be more like one form rather than another. This is simply a category mistake. Of course, that's not to say that the realm of embodied life is unrelated to its inevitable nothingness. If this were the case, then it would be impossible to affirm death at all. It is quite the opposite: we are temporal creatures precisely because we are finite and mortal. But the relationship between embodied life and absolute death is uneven in the sense that the former is utterly absorbed and vanquished by the latter. This view contradicts Bellmer's statements, some quoted above, that the cycles of transformation ensure that whatever is hostile to the self will ultimately be reconciled with it after the death of the self. This ensures that nothing is ever permanently lost to the self, even if in this life Bellmer believes that the living organism is plagued by irrational tendencies. The problem with this logic is that it assumes certain features of the self that no longer apply to it once it transcends embodiment. As already noted, for Bellmer every bodily expression is the result of a displaced energy that results in an image of the body that is never fully reconciled with itself. This implies that self-identical reconciliation is impossible for an embodied self. Hence, for Bellmer, such reconciliation only takes place after the self has perished so that what is same and other can finally merge together under a single principle. So the contradiction is that reconciliation only occurs once the self is no longer bounded by finite parameters, thus implying that we can no longer identify the self as a self. This is in fact the old contradiction of absolute life that has been attributed to all-powerful gods. If these gods are truly all-powerful, all-knowing, and immortal, then it seems invalid to project any limits on them—including the limits of life as we know it. But these limits are how we identify anything at all in the world. Without such limited concepts as color, speed, height, intelligence, brightness, temperature, and so forth, it would be impossible for us to distinguish one thing from another as existing entities. The inference to be drawn, then, is that either the self is bounded and incomplete or it becomes unbounded and therefore dead and nonexistent. And it is in the latter case, for what should be obvious reasons, that the dialectical work of reconciliation no longer applies.

This inference validates the idea, remarked upon at the beginning of the chapter, that the mystery of death challenges all human constructions of meaning. Assuming that we are in fact mortal, that there is nothing within us that is eternal, implies that there is nothing in this world which is permanent. If there were, then it would be possible to form a connection with it in opposition to death. So the line of thought developed above directly contradicts this possibility: there is nothing that we can say or do that puts us in a more harmonious relationship with the very thing that destroys our connections to this world. This logic isn't new; it is the same logic employed by Roland Barthes in his discussion of the *punctum*, that which pierces us, and its power of expansion.[31] To say as he does that there is no "rule of connection" between the *punctum* and the *studium* is to imply, as Derrida has observed, that the other in the same is not to be confined or restricted according to strict boundaries: "As the place of irreplaceable singularity and the unique referential, the *punctum* irradiates and, what is most surprising, lends itself to metonymy. As soon as it allows itself to be drawn into a network of substitutions, it can invade everything, objects as well as effects."[32] The reason given by Derrida for this of expansion is that the *punctum* is dissymmetrical not only to itself but to all things. It is the nonidentity associated with contingency, the irreplaceable, and the *punctum* which makes it impossible to locate these phenomena within a fixed order of any kind. In this way the impact of nonidentity expands in all directions without end; there are limits and structures, but they are always temporary.[33] Entropic affirmation then adds to this insight that it is impossible to affirm this expansiveness to any greater or lesser extent: what is infinitely expansive, as with change, does not provide us with any measurable standard by which we could make such distinctions. It follows that all forms of sublimation embody what is infinite to the same degree. And the self-destructive consequences that are associated with this embodiment, as discussed in reference to the life and death instincts, will likewise remain regardless of how that sublimation takes place. If the affirmation of what we love includes the establishment of social divisions that threaten this same affirmation, then this agonistic orientation of our values cannot be avoided. But this conclusion is not the same as suggesting that all social divisions are necessary, as we know from the tendency to scapegoat. It is precisely such a tendency that gives rise to unnecessary and self-defeating social conflicts. But if all desire is ultimately self-destructive and self-defeating, it is reasonable to ask what it is that distinguishes the erroneous and self-defeating foundation of scapegoating from entropic refraction in general. This will have to be addressed in the next chapter on agonistic pathos.

NOTES

1. Michalski, *The Flame of Eternity*, 84.

2. Although I have addressed this argument and others similar to it more extensively in preceding chapters, it is worth briefly revisiting as new consequences will be drawn from it in the context of the real, the virtual, physical embodiment, the uncanny in Hans Bellmer's art, and suchlike.

3. Jack Kornfield and Gil Fronsdal, *Teachings of the Buddha* (Boston: Shambhala, 2012), 17.

4. Ibid.

5. Not everyone will agree on the semantics here. For some, appearances are illusory only if there is something utterly false about them. But if the process of change

is such that it is always embodied, and thus at least partially real, while nevertheless becoming that which it is not (as with the otherness of death), then strict dichotomies between the real and the illusory are not very useful. It therefore seems appropriate to describe the existence of things as an illusion more in terms of impermanence than absolute non-reality.

6. Jacques Derrida, *Specters of Marx: The State of the Debt, the Work of Mourning, and the New International* (New York: Routledge, 1994), 189; Jacques Derrida, *Spectres de Marx* (Paris: Galilée, 1993), 240.

7. Derrida, *Specters of Marx*, 200; Derrida, *Spectres de Marx*, 254.

8. I have made this argument elsewhere in reverse fashion in terms of our nonidentity: if change proceeds by way of nonidentity as opposed to discrete elements, then it proceeds outward without limitation. That is to say, if we ourselves are constituted in this nonidentical way, then so is the entire world. Hence, put the other way around, if there is something pure within us that never dies, then the world is such that it will always sustain and support us.

9. Derrida, *Of Grammatology*, 154; Derrida, *De la grammatologie*, 215.

10. Derrida, *Of Grammatology*, 158; Derrida, *De la grammatologie*, 220.

11. Derrida et al., *A Taste for the Secret*, 76.

12. Derrida, *Of Grammatology*, 143; Derrida, *De la grammatologie*, 200.

13. On this score, whenever Derrida writes that something like speech promises presence, I will always disagree. It is true that he never makes such observations without also referring to absence and difference, but if it is true that the death instinct is woven into all of our desires, then it's not quite right to claim that we seek presence. This may seem like academic nitpicking, but it becomes very important when considering Derrida's relationship between ethics and difference. So when he makes claims, as we shall see, that the pursuit of absolute presence is linked to different kinds of injustices, we will have to reconsider those claims once it is granted that no such pursuit exists.

14. Foster, *Compulsive Beauty*, 11.

15. Derrida, *Paper Machine*, 138–39.

16. Derrida, *Of Grammatology*, 163; Derrida, *De la grammatologie*, 225.

17. Hans Bellmer, *Little Anatomy of the Physical Unconscious, or the Anatomy of the Image*, trans. Jon Graham (Waterbury Center, VT: Dominion, 2004), 5.

18. It seems apt to describe pain as an example of nonidentity since it presupposes some kind of rupture of the self, as with the piercing of skin. The real and original in Bellmer is therefore already bound up with the artificial.

19. Bellmer, *Little Anatomy of the Physical Unconscious, or the Anatomy of the Image*, 8.

20. Ibid., 9.

21. Ibid., 58.

22. Ibid., 61.

23. Ibid., 66.

24. Sue Taylor, *Hans Bellmer: The Anatomy of Anxiety* (Cambridge, Mass: MIT Press, 2000), 49.

25. Therese Lichtenstein, *Behind Closed Doors: The Art of Hans Bellmer* (Berkeley, CA: University of California Press, 2001), 68.

26. Taylor, *Hans Bellmer: The Anatomy of Anxiety*, 127.

27. Sigmund Freud, *The Uncanny*, trans. David McLintock (New York: Penguin Books, 2003), 142.

28. Foster, *Compulsive Beauty*, 118–19.

29. Lichtenstein, *Behind Closed Doors*, 127–28.

30. Derrida, *Specters of Marx: The State of the Debt, the Work of Mourning, and the New International*, 220; Derrida, *Spectres de Marx*, 278.

31. Roland Barthes, *Camera Lucida: Reflections on Photography*, trans. Richard Howard (New York: Hill and Wang, 1981), 45.

32. Derrida, *Psyche: Inventions of the Other*, 288.

33. What is expansive in this way should be distinguished from how I typically use the term in reference to social values. There is nothing infinite about how those values should be solidified and expanded since they finite and temporary. Rather, they are expansive only in the sense that our needs and desires direct us to connect them up in useful ways with the world around them.

Chapter 7

Agonistic Pathos

The Moot Argument

Derrida argues, successfully I believe, that violence begins with discourse.[1] It begins with discourse in the sense that it is always writing itself by way of supplements, which is to say that it is never one with itself but instead perpetually at odds with its own disappearing condition. It is no wonder that Derrida is skeptical of the divide between animals and humans: every living animal shares in this tragic relationship with an impossible and unthinkable existence. As put forth in the previous chapter, there is no access to a transcendental signified as long as we are immersed in conditions of change and nonidentity. This line of thought diverges, and explicitly so, from the Levinasian view that absolute alterity is open to us without mediation.[2] This is a well-known dispute, but it is one that I wish to say is moot. Whether the infinite is thought to be pure or mediated, transcendent or immanent, in either case all values affirm it equally. And if this is so, then the more pressing question will be that of equal distribution: if all social relationships embody infinite change and nothingness equally, per the entropic argument, then how do we explain the discrepancy between internal and external social divisions? There appear to be, in other words, numerous relationships (between individuals, social groups, etc.) in which the violence and tragedy of death has been projected to the outside, thereby implying that it is not embodied to the same degree regardless of internal and external distinctions. And if not, this would constitute evidence against the case for entropic affirmation made throughout this book. The purpose of this chapter, then, is to make a final argument on behalf of entropic affirmation and resolve this paradoxical attribute of it.

The Transcendent

Levinas begins *Otherwise than Being* with a definition of transcendence: it
is the event of everything that we associate with being (essence, interest, and
sameness) passing over into what is other than being. It is not death, nothingness, or nonbeing, however, since in each case "transcendence" is nothing
more than a dialectical negation immanent to being. But all of the arguments
defended in this book apropos of death and nothingness prove this to be a
mistaken assumption. Death is final, absolute, and irreversible. There is nothing we can do to change this profound and disturbing fact. In this sense, it
is the negations of being more than anything else that pass over into what is
ultimately transcendent.

Nothingness

Levinas continues with the argument that being fills up every moment and
interval of nothingness that would otherwise be said to interrupt its ontological unity. Nothingness is therefore only different in name; in reality it
is continually constituted and reconstituted by the persistence of dialectical
sameness. But in fact this isn't genuine nothingness at all. If it were, what is
it that would be reconstituted by the negations of being? Whatever is reconstituted is by definition not the same thing that was lost to us; it is only a trace
or a memory of what was lost. And what is lost is lost forever as a form of
nothingness.

Memory

Another aspect of the argument is that memory precludes real loss.[3] Although
someone or something is no longer directly in front of us, we are able to
reflect on what is absent in a way that preserves its reality for us. But this
returns us to Derrida's emphasis on the supplement: what is made present
is never made fully present if it depends upon processes of replacement and
substitution. The loss is real, and if it weren't real then no signifying supplement would be required to make it seem less real.

Totality

The above considerations affect several interrelated themes, as I will discuss
here and below. First, if loss is immanent to the negations of being, then
the latter fails to constitute full presence: it is always lacking in some way
or another. This contradicts the notion that being is aligned with systems of
totality. Just the opposite: if it is forever changing and incomplete, then it
precludes any form of social life from achieving oneness with its own aims
and purposes.

Time

Levinas writes that the completion of time is not death but something messianic and eternal.[4] This seems to contradict Dennis King Keenan's equation of the singularity of being mortal with that of infinite time and responsibility.[5] In any event, this too is a mistaken assumption: if death is the converging of life with its inevitable nothingness, then it is in fact the completion of time. It is not a temporary deviation from essence or dialectical negation of the same, but is pure and absolute nothingness.

Indifference

Insofar as Levinas distinguishes the singularity of death from an infinite responsibility toward the other, indifference toward the former is made possible.[6] Indeed, it is required in order to make the patience of responsibility genuine as opposed to being nothing more than a ruse embraced for the benefit of eternal life. Such a motive is more aligned with ontology than it is metaphysics. But if death is the completion of time, then it is impossible to abstract it from ethics, culture, and social relationships. The realm of being open to others is not separate from another realm which is open to change, death, and the nothingness inherent within each of us. To be emotionally invested in anything necessitates that we are also invested in that which will undermine what we love and value. Furthermore, the boundaries between one's own identity and that which we love are in many ways open and porous. This implies, contrary to indifference, that one's concern for the thing or person loved is bound up with a temporality associated not only with the other but also with the self.

Passivity

Levinas also contends that the passivity of obsession is more passive than the passivity of things, since the prime matter of the latter allows for us to construct it in accordance with logos. It is a kind of potency that is susceptible to being designated as this or that sort of thing, as opposed to the passivity of obsession which is prior to any movement of the will or the mind. It thus strips the ego of its pride and "dominating imperialism."[7] This, however, presupposes that matter is fully caught up in such designations. And if we return to earlier arguments made throughout this book apropos of change, it should be clear that matter is always in conflict with itself—so much so that whatever designations we impose upon it will always fail to some degree. And it is this very passivity of being and matter out of which we ourselves are made, thus making it difficult to distinguish our own passivity from its ontological embodiment.

The Given

It is furthermore incorrect to say that being is given to us, say, through vision.[8] The critique is the same as above: if there are no self-identical things in the world then they cannot possibly be given to us in that way. Vision is no more of a dominating sense than any other in this regard, as all of the senses participate in the nonidentity of the world which makes everything in it both present and not present.

The New

Similarly, it is wrong to say that being does not give rise to anything truly new. This is implied when it is argued that the infinity of the existent, which comes about in a refusal of totalization, is what produces a real commencement. And so what does not produce this real commencement is the indetermination of what is simply there, that is, the anarchy and the anonymity of the *il y a*. The above arguments show this to be false insofar as transcendence is not to be confined to any particular existent: it is pervasive throughout being in all of its shapes and forms. This means that every moment of being is not only immanent but also outside of itself. There is change at every level, and thus things disappear and new things arise.

Ulysses

It cannot be the case, then, that the so-called adventures of thought and action are destined to return to their place of origin. There is no such home. There is only change that takes us further and further away from ourselves in the sense that we become precisely that which is nothing at all. The realm of being does not fold back on itself dialectically speaking. It does not continually absorb us until we become one with all of the world and the universe. It is both identity and nonidentity, fullness and emptiness, real and unreal, present and not present. It is all of these things because the new is not to be confined to any particular kind of reality or existent: what happens today has never happened before. That's not to deny order and structure and stability, but the patterns that coexist with change are no less temporal than anything else in the world. It is therefore a false dichotomy to separate ontology from metaphysics on the assumption that the former is guided by a deterministic teleology.

The Face and the Mask

Another false dichotomy is the one posited between the face and the mask. What is unique about oneself is not separate from being, and thus it doesn't pierce through being as if the latter were nothing more than a mask. There isn't infinity on one side and being on the other. If we are unique at all, it is because we disappear from the world without being absorbed within all of its changes. And it is the multitude of endless changes that puts into question strict limits or boundaries between the inside and the outside. In this way, the face and the mask merge together without therefore becoming fully unified.

The Ego

The above conclusion is in agreement with the view that the ego fails to coincide with itself, but the set of reasons given for it are based on change and nothingness rather than false dichotomies.

Infinity

All of the above arguments apply to infinity as well. When it is thus said that the production of infinity is made possible by a certain disproportion between that infinity and its idea, this shouldn't be limited by any false dichotomies. The endless changes and negations of being are likewise produced by way of limits that expose a certain disproportion between those changes and what is changing. There is a process and movement of change that exceeds all limits but only insofar as those limits make change possible. Hence there is always a disproportion between one thing and another, even beyond our ideas of infinity.

Intentionality

Likewise, the relationship between the subject and the object should always be defined in terms of non-adequation. There is no operation of intentionality apart from this kind of relationship. It's misleading, then, to establish a dichotomy between the idea of infinity and that of intentionality when every single relationship is one of non-adequation between the subject and the object. This is a similar point as the one above apropos of the given: there is absolutely nothing given to consciousness if what is meant by the given is something purely self-identical. All feelings and perceptions undergo change, which implies that they necessarily overflow themselves—as Levinas says of the idea of infinity.

Thematization

And if all feelings and perceptions undergo change, then they resist thematization in the same way that anything infinite should be said to resist thematization. They do not have a strict beginning or end. They are not defined, or should not be defined, as discrete units of consciousness. Hence they are not given to us in this way, as self-identical units or properties. And if they cannot be given to us in this way, then they cannot be situated as themes within a larger narrative structure that makes all things fully present. So when it is said that infinity resists thematization, this logic should be applied to all aspects of being, reality, and consciousness equally. This is in fact the argument of entropic affirmation.

Things of the World

All of the above arguments, or something similar to them, have been made by Derrida. He thus writes that if we question the Levinasian position that the things of the world do not provide real resistance to the ego or the same, then everything else that follows from this will also be put into question. These things provide us with a resistance that is much more than a temporary obstacle: whatever we do to make them conform to our wishes they nonetheless embody the same nonidentity that pervades everything.

Work

Hence the resistance that the world provides in relationship to work is not simply a moment of the same or the ego's economy.[9] It is not a transitional form of alterity, one that poses an obstacle on the way to forming a greater totality of synthesis with the subject. Our relationship with the other doesn't begin with a movement away from being, work, or history, but is immanent in everything that we do.

Need and Desire

As intimated earlier, this line of thought has several implications. If otherness is pervasive throughout all things, then need and desire will never completely realize themselves. If the embodiment of life is itself a form of alterity grounded in a world without either beginning or end, then every satisfaction will have to be incomplete and temporary. In this way there is no metaphysical desire apart from that which aims for its own self-destruction; there is no realm that exists on its own independently of change. And it is change that brings about the inevitable destruction of life which likewise destroys need and desire.

Teleology

Related to the last point, the aim of either need or desire cannot be simply instrumental: they do not seek only to fulfill ends that complete them. There is always a self-destructive aspect that cannot be removed or abstracted from the teleology of our goals. Returning to arguments made throughout this book, if all things undergo change then the principle of nonidentity (as well as alterity, otherness, heterogeneity, the abyss, and so forth) applies to our goals as much as anything else in the world. That implies that the realm of desire is not something separate from a drive which puts into action its own self-destruction. In this way metaphysical desire cannot be separated from ontological desire: in all cases our relationship to the outside, to what is exterior and limitless, is conditioned by the nothingness of death.

The Supplement

Derrida thus argues that the supplement is placed in the void or the abyss. There is no final context for desire, signification, speech, writing, or anything at all. Every relationship with the outside is by way of a supplement that makes present what can never be made present. So there is no direct, unmediated form of communication with the other. There is no speech in this sense. There is only supplemental writing that brings us together even as it keeps us infinitely separated.

Irreducibility

What is most irreducible about experience, then, cannot be our orientation toward the other as a living other, whether human or otherwise. It is true that the other in this sense is infinitely other. It is also true that this orientation is irreducible. But it is not as if this is the most fundamental explanation of what it is that makes the other absolutely other. The explanation does not begin separately from the abyss that makes all forms of communication mediated and supplemental. The abyss pervades us, but it also extends outwardly in all directions without any permanent limits or boundaries. The things of this world that are not alive are changing and disappearing too, which makes them infinitely distant from us—even when we hold them in our hands. What makes them irreducible to possession, then, is not unique to humans.

Neutralization

If the above reasoning is correct, then being does not neutralize the other. For it to do so, there would have to be a strict dichotomy between the two in which the former had nothing to do with the latter. In that case, privileging that which is purely objective would in fact constitute a reduction of the infinite relation to something instrumental. But there is no such dichotomy, and that's important. The realm of being is pervaded with otherness, heterogeneity, and difference. That's not to say that the realms of the animate and the inanimate are entirely the same, or that we should treat one no differently than the other. That's not the argument here. But what *is* being said here is that an acknowledgment of the nonidentity and change that is everywhere in being does nothing to take away from the nonidentity of social life.

The Finite

What this really amounts to is Derrida's argument that we cannot designate the infinite apart from the finite: every metaphor that is used to represent the former ineluctably makes use of the latter.[10] Terms such as height, exteriority, or the outside exemplify this tendency perfectly. In each case what is identified as infinite is nevertheless couched in terms that remind us of spatial representations. And in this manner what is infinite is mixed in with what is finite, limited, and ephemeral. For us humans, the infinite is only relevant to us as finite beings with finite dimensions. That's not to say that it doesn't transcend us. If we take infinite change as an example, it should be clear from previous arguments that it pervades all things even as it moves beyond them. In the second chapter this is what I referred to as infinite embodiment: it is the paradoxical condition of a finite existence open to that which is absolutely all-pervasive.

Self-Interest

Another implication of the immanence (and transcendence) of otherness in all things is that we are never motivated simply and only by self-interest. Insofar as we are nonidentical beings, all values will embody this fact in everything that we do. This runs counter to the line of thought, defended by Cheryl L. Hughes for example, that infinite responsibility is prior to that of self-preservation.[11] This is not the case if the two are simultaneously embodied in *all* values: on the one hand we tend to pursue that which gives our values the best chance at survival, but on the other we also put into motion the very opposite, that is, that which limits and destroys those values. This wouldn't be the case if the life and death instincts could be separated from one another, but as I argued in Chapter 6 they are indeed one and the same. To pursue what is to our advantage, then, is to also embrace the infinite movement of change that will destroy us.

Conflict

This complicates the inference from self-interest to conflict and war. It may be that there is something about ontology that implies social divisions, as I will suggest below, but this has less to do with self-interest than it does with the connection between life and death. Furthermore, there is no reason to think that this connection automatically leads to the kind of social divisions that are unnecessarily violent. It is always possible to avoid military warfare, for example, by emphasizing diplomatic solutions. But these solutions have nothing to do with overcoming self-interest in accordance with our infinite responsibilities.

The Moot Point, Again

Much of the critique outlined above has already been articulated by Derrida in some fashion or another: there is no transcendental signified, discourse is inherently violent, alterity is immanent to being, presence and absence are bound together, and so forth. The moot point, though, has to do with the better solution to conflict: is it correct to infer that being more receptive to the infinity (i.e., heterogeneity and difference) within discourse, as opposed to the Levinasian version, is what helps us to mitigate unnecessary forms of violence? The argument of this book is that it simply doesn't matter if the Levinasian view is refuted: one version of difference supplanting another does not get us any closer to Derrida's goals. The deconstructive attitude is that the movement of language is likewise the movement of a certain kind of violence, a certain kind of finitude that is always in conflict with itself, but whether we say that infinity is inside or outside of discourse it remains the fact that all values are equally receptive to it.

Chance and Incompetence

The entropic argument should therefore be applied to both conceptions, since in either case we can draw no inferences from receptivity and openness to the mitigation of war, violence, and scapegoating. When Brian Schroeder contends, from a Levinasian perspective, that the affirmation of radical chance, risk, and spontaneity will help us to achieve more peaceful relations,[12] it is difficult to imagine how chance is any more aligned with one affirmation rather than another—since all values embody it equally.[13] And when Nick Mansfield makes nearly the same argument,[14] except from a Derridean point of view, the response should be the same: it is difficult to know which values are more open than others to the absolute nature of risk and incompetence when that absoluteness is absolutely everywhere.

Metaphysics

For this reason, which has been developed at greater length in preceding chapters, Derrida is incorrect to argue that writing is more "metaphysical" than speech.[15] The writer does not "absent himself" anymore through writing than through any other means. He does not address himself to the other to any greater degree than he would through proximity, persecution, or vulnerability. In each case we can always respond, as we should, that what is meant by metaphysics is either finite, infinite, or some combination of the two. In the finite case, it is a debatable question whether a specific situation calls for being more open and receptive. Sometimes it will and sometimes it will not.

And in the two cases involving infinity, it remains impossible to say which values embody it more than others.

Presence

It is likewise incorrect to suggest that we desire or long for presence even as it is deferred. If we are absent from ourselves, then this is true in everything that we do and say. It is not as if we desire or search for what is always out of reach; we do not search for it at all. The self-destructive aspect of all desire ensures that what we truly pursue, sometimes unconsciously, is a life pervaded with beautiful pain and tragedy.

The Same

That also holds for the view that philosophy, in some of its variations, seeks to absorb the other into the same. If this were true, it would imply that that there is indeed a desire on the part of some to transform what is the same into a systematic totality. This would be the desire for complete presence. But there is no such desire as long as it is remembered that we never seek or desire anything apart from death, as put forth in the chapter "Dolls and Death." As long as every desire is bound up with entropic affirmation, we only desire things on the condition that they are finite, changing, and temporal. It is true that we may say the opposite, that what we want is to have absolute knowledge and absolute life, but what we say is not always consistent with what we truly desire—as the latter is oftentimes repressed or unconscious.

Change

The entropic argument made thus far depends on a certain assumption that change is real, infinite, and absolute. Although the reasons for making this assumption have been provided in earlier chapters, it may prove helpful to briefly rehearse them in an effort to show the overall, basic trajectory of thought leading us to the final conclusions of this chapter.

Observation

Probably the most common sense reason for this assumption is derived from the simple observation that we see change all around us. It seems real enough, and the burden of proof should weigh heavily on any arguments to the contrary. Nonetheless, it doesn't hurt to reinforce what should be empirically obvious with further arguments underscoring the nature and reality of what we observe daily.

Oneness

One way of showing that change is real, other than through simple observation, is by refuting claims that it is not real. One such claim is based on the view that all things are ultimately one, which would negate the possibility of change since what is changing presupposes a transition from one form of reality to another. Oneness and self-division, that is to say, are incompatible. But if this is right, it becomes difficult to explain how the experience of change arises. Either it is real or illusory. In the first case, the idea that all things are one is invalidated. But in the second case, the illusion is by definition set against the rest of reality since it is not an accurate portrayal of it. And if it is set against it, then reality is no longer strictly speaking one with itself. So it doesn't matter if experience is said to be illusory in some way. Whether it is a dream or pure hallucination, in all cases it implies the existence of a world divided against itself.

Dualism

The problem with the above account is that strict ontological unity precludes the possibility of any change whatsoever. Dualism gets around this by splitting up the world into two separate realities: the changing and the unchanging, the perfect and the imperfect, the material and the immaterial. If these two forms of existence are in fact distinct and separate, then it can be maintained that the eternal realm is absolutely real while the transitory one is not. But if this distinction is valid, it becomes difficult once again to explain how it is that the experience of change arises. If there is something within each of us that is eternal—as with an immortal soul—such that by definition it cannot be changed by temporal circumstances, then it cannot experience anything at all which would contradict this assumption. In this way, it is impossible for the eternal soul to experience change as that would constitute a transition from one state or experience to another. That temporal creatures such as ourselves do in fact experience change therefore makes it implausible that the underlying reality of that change is either one with itself or eternal.

Limits

It might be agreed that change is real but not unlimited. This would be the case if it transpired by way of discrete elements, since those elements would not in themselves undergo any transformation during the process of change. All that would take place, then, would be the rearrangement of such elements, but they themselves would remain self-identical. This, however, presupposes something untenable, namely, that there is nothing in this world which is an example of nonidentical change. In fact, there are plenty of such examples, as with anyone's experience of a temporal moment giving way to the next. If that moment were frozen in time, then we would experience it as it is with full clarity and distinctness. But in fact there are many examples to the contrary, in which the moment of time experienced is already becoming that which it is not—a new moment of existence and temporality. And once we have identified something nonidentical in this way, it is impossible to impose limits on it since what is nonidentical is precisely that sort of phenomenon which breaks down and overflows such limits.

Illusion

As with the monism argument above, it might once again be said in response that what is perceived to be nonidentical, such as a particular experience, is itself an illusion—one which focuses our attention away from the discrete elements and patterns that are the true source of change. But it doesn't matter to the nonidentity argument whether the experience is illusory or not. Even an illusion has some reality to it qua illusion, so its nonidentity still counts as a portion of existence that fails to be one with itself.

Loss

It might then be agreed that change is real and unlimited, but not furthermore absolute. This would imply that death is merely a transition from one state of things to another, without there being any hint that an actual and absolute loss of life also takes place. But if this were the case, then the entire transition from life to death would have to be experienced in an entirely positive way. It would be a transition from a life trapped by the finite contours of the ego to a form of existence reunited with the infinite forces of nature that are all-pervasive. Whatever is inside of us, whatever instincts or forces, would feel reinforced by this return to our infinite source of life and energy. This model of change therefore seems inadequate to what many of us in fact experience in the face of loss and death—fear, sadness, and anxiety. So the fact that these emotions exist, and aren't entirely misguided, suggests to us that loss is both real and absolute.

Infinite Embodiment

The above considerations lead us to the idea of infinite embodiment, which is the idea that the unlimited aspects of change and death are embodied in everything that we do. If there are no permanent limits to nonidentity, then everything finite is pervaded with the alterity of change that destroys all things. There is no separation of one from the other: it is change, otherness, and multiplicity all the way down. It is true that there are boundaries in life, without which we could not survive, but these are precarious boundaries for the very simple reason that they are finite and changing. Their temporary consolidation therefore presupposes a fundamental openness to that which overtakes and destroys them.

Entropic Embodiment

This idea is immanent to the one above: if the unlimited is embodied in all actions and values, then the latter are ultimately self-destructive. Certain caveats have to be made, but this argument is essentially another way of articulating the death drive. The caveats that should be added will be discussed shortly.

Entropic Affirmation

While the ontological scope of entropic embodiment extends beyond the realm of social values, the latter cannot be separated from the former. Every example of a social value, in other words, involves the process of self-destruction that is associated with entropic temporality. In fact, it *is* this process of change and self-destruction. In this manner, insofar as every example of a social value affirms itself, which is to say that it affirms its own reality and embodiment, it likewise affirms its entropic condition.

Openness and Closure

The idea of entropic affirmation, then, is that we cannot affirm life apart from those things which cannot be separated from it: change, mortality, absence, otherness, difference, and so forth. But another aspect of this idea is that it precludes distinctions between values in terms of openness and closure. If there is, after all, something infinite about otherness, then by definition it cannot be measured. This means that all forms of existence, including social values, are equally exposed to it. It also means that our values will be equally removed from it, insofar as they all fall infinitely short of it. There are no degrees of difference in terms of either affirmation or rejection.

Simulation

If there is no difference between openness and closure vis-à-vis infinite otherness, then the postmodern emergence of the simulacrum is a myth. We are not at risk of too much assimilation if what we have in mind is absolute alterity, since the latter exceeds all forms of virtual reality equally. Of course, if what we have in mind is something different, as with *specific* forms of alterity, then it behooves us to think more seriously about issues of openness and closure. But these issues, for the very reason that they are specific in nature, will always be contextual: sometimes openness will be justified, other times not. The very fact that we make decisions, deciding for or against a certain path, implies that we embrace closure to some degree. In this way closure, assimilation, and the simulacrum fail to be intrinsically problematic, for either they are (1) mythical, or (2) real phenomena whose value depends upon contextual factors.

Catastrophe

One of the first consequences of entropic affirmation, then, is that we should be wary of claims that the rejection of otherness, via the simulacrum, lends itself to catastrophe. In general, what is being suggested by these claims is that there is a predictive connection between our disavowal of change and death and the tendency toward war, violence, scapegoating, and cultural self-destruction. But if there are no greater or lesser modes of disavowal in relation to irreducible otherness, the argument falls flat.

Social Equality

Not all versions of irreducible otherness identify it with change and death; others align it more closely with the value of social equality. In such cases the catastrophic trajectory begins with a different premise but follows the same logic: the disavowal of what is inherently valuable within each of us, as with the fact of life itself, is what creates a greater likelihood of violent and self-destructive consequences.

Precarious Life

If we begin, for example, with the apprehension of life as inherently pre-carious, as Butler does, it would be accurate to infer that this apprehension applies to all life equally. Indeed, at the purely ontological or metaphysical level, this is equivalent to the premise of entropic embodiment. But equality in terms of our primordial condition does not lend itself to the kind of equal-ity that Butler seeks: simply because we share in something ontologically does not mean that this equality also applies to our social values. To avoid the naturalistic fallacy that seems immanent here, Butler argues that a proper description of precarious life extends beyond the primordial to include the fact that we are socially dependent upon one another. In this way what is irreducible need not be restricted to one level or another but can be applied to both: to deny our dependence on others is to deny an absolutely irreducible fact concerning all of us, and this fact is not only existential but furthermore social, ethical, and political. This turn of the argument, however, doesn't do much for us—as the proof for an absolute social value such as equality should not be derived from conditions of mutual dependence which are themselves highly variable.

Reducibility

So there is a problem in the argument that some values are irreducible. If it means that they cannot be reduced to anything at all, this is false insofar as entropic embodiment ensures that they will inevitably be reduced to nothingness. Assuming that this principle of self-destruction is correct, it satisfies the strict definition of reducibility which involves a transformation from one condition to another. But if it means only that it cannot undergo such a transformation on a specified level of reality, as with social reality, then this is false whenever this does in fact happen. So if we return to the value of social equality, one which is often connected to conditions of mutual dependence, it is difficult not to observe that this value is likely to undergo processes of transformation insofar as the conditions of mutual dependence are themselves open to different forms of actualization. In some cases, they will be associated with a relatively high level of social equality, as can be found between two friends who enjoy being with one another regardless of political or business interests. In others, however, they will be associated more closely with the social elements of power, hierarchy, status, money, and so forth—as takes place in business, government, the military, family relations, and so forth. Social equality, then, cannot fulfill the conditions of an irreducible value simply by connecting it to the phenomenon of mutual dependence, since the latter is susceptible to taking on at least some degree of inequality. If, in other words, there were an irreducible link between equality and mutual dependence, then this susceptibility would be impossible.

Inferences

If the alterity of life, including its precariousness, does not justify a specific set of values, it might therefore be inferred that we do away with this concept. But this inference is too quick. As we shall soon see, while it is true that entropic embodiment precludes the justification of specific values, as with equality, kindness, or generosity, it nonetheless structures all of our values in a way that should not be ignored.

Expansive Singularities

If the infinity of death, per the entropic argument, is affirmed in everything we do, then this will have a real influence on the orientation of our social values. To the extent that we value something, we desire that it be preserved and strengthened. But there is a limit on this expansive quality of social values since we also affirm their unavoidable destruction. Indeed, this is what is meant by the singularity of what we value: insofar as it is affirmed to the point of nothingness, it undermines processes of assimilation. What dies, that is to say, cannot be fully understood or systematized. And we ourselves affirm this in all of our values. So whatever it is that we wish to expand we also wish to destroy, and this will have consequences in terms of agonistic pathos and the creation of social divisions.

Ideal Life

Another way of stating the above argument is to add that we do not pursue or desire the sort of life that exists without obstacles. It is not enough, in the critique of various social systems, to say that the ideal life is imaginary. Not only is it imaginary, but furthermore it is impossible to desire as long as it remains true that desire is always bound up with the affirmation of its own dissolution. The social and political critique, then, that some values are nefarious insofar as they perpetuate the dream of an absolute or ideal life is therefore invalid; per the entropic argument, there are no values which pursue this kind of dream. This view is compatible with the fact that in some particular domains of life we take up fewer challenges and obstacles than in others. A chess player, for example, may not take up the challenges of playing piano, just as the pianist may not take up the challenges of mountain biking. In any case, the moral imperative to engage the difficulties of life is either too broad or too narrow. If we have in mind life in general, then as we have seen above it is impossible to affirm life without also affirming a tremendous obstacle to one's goals—considering that entropic affirmation ultimately brings about their destruction. But if we have in mind a specific set of challenges, as with chess or playing basketball, there is no reason to think that all such difficulties should be pursued. Depending on the context, some challenges will help us to expand our values while others remain irrelevant to our passions, desires, and goals.

Bio-Power

The same can also be said of bio-power: there is no system of values which has as its single, pervasive aim the heightening of life forces. Again, in the general sense of life this is impossible since we also affirm the destruction of those systems, values, and forces. While in the more specific domains of life the heightening of one goal typically presupposes the diminishment of another: if I heighten my abilities and skills as a philosopher, mountain biker, and chess player then I will likely diminish my abilities in other domains. So in the specific sense of life's possibilities the imperative isn't to maximize life but to maximize one of its versions—which by definition minimizes other versions. Hence there are two fundamental reasons for rejecting the view that modern power is guided by nothing more than the maximization of life. First, it is impossible to desire the ideal life set apart from death if we also affirm the latter: one drive presupposes the other in everything that we do and value. And second, the maximization of a specific version of life necessarily minimizes other versions: if choices are real, as opposed to being all-embracing, then they not only maximize certain goals and possibilities but minimize an infinity of others.

Paradoxes

Foucault is thus incorrect to claim that there is a paradox of bio-power whenever it lends itself to war, conflict, and destruction. If it were pervaded through and through with calculation and life-enhancement, then of course it would strike us as surprising if it nonetheless lent itself to great devastation. But this is a paradox of Foucault's own making. There is no system of power focused solely on optimizing life. As soon as we recognize that the desire to expand our values is necessarily bound up with an antithetical drive to destroy them, the possibilities of conflict no longer seem so unusual or paradoxical.

Nature

The argument that all values affirm and maximize life to the same degree is counterintuitive, so it may be helpful to make a comparison. If we think of the same argument in terms of nature, for instance, then the underlying logic becomes clear: there is nothing in this world which is any more or any less a part of nature than anything else. A small piece of dirt is just as much an expression of the natural world as, say, the sky, the moon, a living person, or a large building. It makes no difference since nature permeates all of these things equally. And the same is true for the maximization of life: unless we have already defined it in reference to a specific set of goals and purposes, all distinctions fade away. In every case imaginable, from crickets and antelopes to the life of the poor, the middle class, or the extremely rich, whatever is valued and affirmed is an equal manifestation of life in general.

Entropic Refraction

What has been established, then, is that even though values are somewhat instrumental and expansive, they are also self-destructive. And as intimated above, this has implications for how we approach their conflictual aspects. We should no longer contend, for example, that these aspects have something to do with an immortality drive—as the latter simply does not exist. Neither are they related to greater or lesser openness to death and otherness, that is, the concrete antitheses of immortality, as the concept of entropic affirmation precludes such differences. Instead, it is entropic refraction which helps us to understand the inherently agonistic orientation of social values.

Multiplicity

To the extent that such values are truly self-destructive, they will never seek out full integration with the social world around them. The latter would do away with everything singular and self-destructive, thereby contradicting the overall trajectory of those values. At the very least, then, it should be agreed that this trajectory favors the multiplicity of social values rather than their unity and assimilation.

Agonistic Relationships

Multiplicity, however, does not by itself imply that our values are either ago-nistic or conflictual.[16] There are many ways of thinking through multiplicity so that different social values and ways of life remain open to one another. But due to the self-destructive nature of those values, such openness has a limit. Let's say, as a thought experiment, that the entire social field embraced multiplicity without any of the values involved posing a threat to our own. In that case, if there truly were no threats, then it would have to be said that the entire social field of such values would in every way support our own— for what does not pose a threat to the existence of my values ultimately supports them. Intuitively this strikes us as a false dichotomy, but in truth even the slightest gap of temporality and difference between values ensures that they will perish. So either they are fully integrated with all others or exposed to the embodiment of life that brings about their destruction. Hence the affirmation of that embodiment, which is the primordial condition of social life, leads to entropic refraction, that is, the affirmation of other values and social systems that pose a threat to our own. When we affirm our own values, that is to say, we also affirm, sometimes without knowing it, the existence of a social field that brings to an end whatever we love, need, and desire.

Conscious and Unconscious Affirmations

It would seem plausible that if we affirm and put into action the dissolution of our own values that we would know this to be the case. But of course it is possible, via cognitive dissonance, for a discrepancy to arise. It may be that what I affirm is one thing while what I *think* I affirm remains something else. This is particularly true vis-à-vis entropic refraction, since it comes about as an indirect consequence of entropic affirmation. In this way, if cognitive dis-sonance is possible for the latter, then it is even more so for the former, thus explaining the last sentence of the last section in which it is put forth that we are not always aware of the kind of social field that we embrace through our actions and values.

Potential Equilibrium

One suggestion for getting around the necessity of agonistic relationships is by pointing to the possibility of shared responsiveness. In this scenario, the threats to social life are relegated to the natural realm in such a way that they are acknowledged without thereby asserting that we ourselves must exacerbate the situation. This argument seems to be compatible with entropic affirmation insofar as it allows for the fact that we affirm death and nothingness, but avoids the implication that this involves the creation of social divisiveness as long we act collectively in response to natural threats and dangers. But this assumes, as put forth in Chapter 5, a purely defensive attitude toward death, one which projects it outside all social values. But if the latter are themselves a manifestation of entropic embodiment, then they do not merely resist death but actively bring it about through the creation of divisions in the larger social field.

Scapegoating

Insofar as the values that we affirm necessarily lead to some kind of entropic refraction, whereby social divisions are created through the affirmation of expansive singularities, it follows that not all such divisions are equivalent to scapegoating. If they were, which is another way of suggesting that all of them could be avoided, then the above goal of an equilibrium of social life would be less idealistic. But there are plenty of examples in which we must take up the challenge of an agonistic relationship without that necessarily implying that we have scapegoated the other. Indeed, being able to recognize when this challenge is real as opposed to being the result of propaganda is absolutely crucial to the flourishing of any social group. If we look at recent political events in 2017, for example, it should be clear that the proclivity of President Trump to scapegoat any person or group who doesn't blindly follow him poses a grave risk to the security and reputation of the United States of America. On the other hand, he continues to overlook real threats to his country when he dismisses Russian interference in the 2016 US elections as a media witch hunt.

Agonistic Pathos

What the above arguments ultimately show is that entropic affirmation leads to agonistic pathos. As long as the life and death drives are ultimately united so that we never affirm one without the other, our social values should be described in terms of expansive singularities. This implies, as put forth already, that they cannot be affirmed without putting into effect self-destructive consequences. And if this is correct, then it follows that those values do not seek full integration with the social field around them, as that would contradict the premise of entropic affirmation. If they are truly self-destructive, then they themselves help to create the conditions which ultimately separate them from the larger social field. This is why it was argued above that our values do not merely hold a passive relationship to death, but actively bring it about through entropic refraction. It is the latter phenomenon which lends itself to values being opposed to one another. Of course it is also true, insofar as those values are expansive, that they seek out harmonious connections with the world around them. But there is a limit to this process insofar as those values are also self-destructive. And it is this limit that ensures that our values are not fully sustained by the social field in which they exist, as there are real threats and dangers to their existence. Moreover, if the values themselves help to create this limit, then there is at least some identification with their opposition. In this manner the term "agonistic pathos" seems appropriate.

Sublimation

Agonistic values need not express themselves through militaristic confrontations. When possible, they should be sublimated toward goals which help them to flourish as much as possible, especially within the context of culture and economics. But it should be remembered that if these values are genuinely divisive, then the values which oppose them will constitute no less of a threat for being sublimated. As there is no transcendence above or beyond entropic affirmation, whatever social values embody and sublimate it do so with all of the same self-destructive tendencies.

Method

The agonistic orientation of values elaborated above has been influenced by a number of thinkers, but I would like to think that it also makes its own mark. It is my contention that no other author highlights the immediate relevance of infinite otherness to our values without making that relevance depend upon the openness of those values to what transcends them. If this fails to be correct, then whatever follows from the insight of entropic affirmation will not be distinguished from rival theories and methodologies.

The Hierarchy of Types

Nietzsche stipulates a will to power that likewise lends itself to conflictual and agonistic values. But these values are then distinguished from one another on the basis of their relationship to life and nature, in the sense that some of them are more hostile than others to their own primordial condition.

These values are then deemed to be anti-nature and anti-life.[17] What was argued in Chapter 4, however, is that there is no such distinction between the will to power and the will to nothingness. There is no affirmation of life that embodies a will toward the perfect life, as with the will to nothingness, since the values associated with that affirmation would be expansive as well as self-destructive. And it is the latter tendency which exposes the will to nothingness as something less than a will to anti-nature and anti-life perfection.

The Constitutive Outside

I have also expressed my agreement with Matthias Fritsch that the creation of a constitutive outside does not necessarily lend itself to agonistic relationships. When Chantal Mouffe draws such a connection, then, it should be asked why it is that the constitutive outside couldn't instead be associated with friend-friend relationships instead of competitive or adversarial ones.[18] This is Fritsch's question when he writes that there is no reason to assume that a friendship is automatically totalizing.[19] But the argument that begins with a constitutive outside is different from another that highlights entropic affirmation, for in the latter case it is impossible to avoid the consequences of values understood as expansive singularities. Those are the types of values that introduce breaks into the social field. And if those breaks are completely harmless, then they do not in truth represent the tendency toward entropic refraction. So if there is a limit to the expansive qualities of our values, then it follows that what they affirm includes not only their harmonious connections within the social field but also a tendency toward fragmentation and dissolution.

The Death Instinct

The last point applies not only to Mouffe but to any theory emphasizing the positivity of values apart from their destructive tendencies. Utilitarianism and pragmatism, insofar as they focus on constructive results, must therefore be included in this group. Of course, it's not as if James, Dewey, and other pragmatists ignore the tragic aspects of social life, but their account of what we need and desire leaves out the self-destructive tendency to undermine whatever constitutes our primary self-interest.

The Life Instinct

The same can also be said for the life instinct: based on a variety of arguments made throughout this book, it is not reducible to an external influence on processes of self-dissolution. Freud makes this mistake when he writes that the instinct toward death was originally quite simple, until it was eventually sidetracked by external influences which compelled it to sustain its own existence for longer periods of time.[20] This line of thought presumes that there are strict boundaries between the inside and the outside, as if what keeps an instinct bound together has nothing to do with its own reality, while in fact the self-destructive instinct could not exist in the first place if it weren't already motivated to sustain and perpetuate itself.

Internal and External Divisions

The method employed in these pages, then, challenges the presumption of a sharp dividing line between the inside and the outside: whatever is affirmed in our values is always pervaded by the infinite processes of change which overturn those same set of values. But at the same time it would be unwise to believe for this reason that all such distinctions are rendered meaningless, as that would transform everything identified as temporary and finite into something that is one with all things. The latter is not likely to be true given various arguments put forth in chapters 3 and 6. But if all social values embody the absence of death and otherness to the same degree, then how is it that such distinctions are still maintained? Isn't there a paradox in holding the view that all values affirm otherness equally even as those same values embody differential relationships with one another? However, while it is true that every aspect and every moment of refraction embodies infinite otherness equally, it doesn't follow from this that what is infinite completely does away with all distinctions. To the contrary, what has been argued elsewhere, particularly in Chapter 6, is that every affirmation of infinite otherness presupposes a supplement that is at odds with a complete reconciliation of all differences. And this line of thought avoids the potential paradoxes and contradictions stated above by highlighting two different kinds of relations: one which is infinite and thus embodies that infinity to the same degree as any other infinite relation, and another which compares the infinite relations to one another in terms of their finite aspects. This is possible since infinite embodiment presupposes both infinity as well as finitude, as argued in Chapter 2, which implies that its finite aspects can indeed be compared to anything else in the world that is finite without that comparison immediately dissolving into a form of absolute unity or nothingness.

NOTES

1. Derrida, *Writing and Difference*, 117; Derrida, *L'écriture et la différence*, 172.

2. Miller, *For Derrida*, 114–15.

3. Emmanuel Levinas, *Otherwise Than Being, or Beyond Essence*, trans. Alphonso Lingis (Pittsburgh, PA: Duquesne University Press, 1998), 9; Emmanuel Levinas, *Autrement qu'etre, ou au-dela de l'essence* (The Hague: Nijhoff, 1978), 22.

4. Emmanuel Levinas, *Totality and Infinity: An Essay on Exteriority*, trans. Alphonso Lingis (Pittsburgh, PA: Duquesne University Press, 1969), 284–85; Emmanuel Levinas, *Totalité et infini* (The Hague: Nijhoff, 1961), 318.

5. Dennis King Keenan, *Death and Responsibility: The "Work" of Levinas* (Albany, NY: SUNY Press, 1999), 79.

6. Emmanuel Levinas and Nidra Poller, *Humanism of the Other* (Champagne, Il: University of Illinois Press, 2003), 27.

7. Levinas, *Otherwise Than Being, or Beyond Essence*, 110; Levinas, *Autrement qu'etre, ou au-dela de l'essence*, 175.

8. Levinas, *Totality and Infinity: An Essay on Exteriority*, 194; Levinas, *Totalité et infini*, 211.

9. Derrida, *Writing and Difference*, 94; Derrida, *L'écriture et la différence*, 139.

10. Derrida, *Writing and Difference*, 114; Derrida, *L'écriture et la différence*, 168.

11. Cheryl L Hughes, "The Primacy of Ethics: Hobbes and Levinas," *Continental Philosophy Review* 31, no. 1 (1998): 79.

12. Brian Schroeder, *Altared Ground: Levinas, History, and Violence* (London: Routledge, 1996), 146.

13. That isn't to deny that there are differences between values when looked at from a finite perspective. But then it all depends on context: embracing a religious tradition may put someone at risk more in one country rather than another, and this risk can be observed and measured to some degree. And once we have in mind particular forms of chance, otherness, or difference, it's always an open question whether these forms should be embraced or not. So the argument that we should affirm chance is invalid for either one of two reasons: (1) it is meant in the radical, infinite sense, in which case there are no greater or lesser affirmations; or (2) it is actually meant in the less radical sense of something finite and specific, in which case it is not always true that we should affirm it.

14. Nick Mansfield, "Refusing Defeatism: Derrida, Decision and Absolute Risk," *Social Semiotics* 16, no. 3 (2006): 478–80.

15. Derrida, *Writing and Difference*, 102; Derrida, *L'écriture et la différence*, 150–51.

16. I have been using the adjectives agonistic and conflictual somewhat interchangeably. Not everyone will agree to this kind of overlapping conceptualization. But if agonistic social values include something threatening to our way of life, as I articulate shortly, then a strict dichotomy between competition and conflict will blind us to real threats.

17. Friedrich Nietzsche, *Twilight of the Idols and the Anti-Christ*, trans. R. J. Hollingdale (New York: Penguin, 1888), 52–57.

18. Chantal Mouffe, *The Democratic Paradox* (New York: Verso, 2000), 12–13.

19. Fritsch, "Antagonism and Democratic Citizenship (Schmitt, Mouffe, Derrida)," 185.

20. Sigmund Freud, *Beyond the Pleasure Principle*, trans. James Strachey (New York: W. W. Norton & Company, 1961), 46.

Chapter 8

Questions and Objections

Is the underlying starting point of thanato-vitalism the concept of infinity or entropic affirmation?

The first concept, sometimes referred to as infinite embodiment, is the primary assumption underlying the method of thanato-vitalism. It states that infinite change is embodied in all things. However, this by itself is not an original insight and therefore cannot be said to orient the trajectory of the method in a distinctive manner. The latter task falls to entropic affirmation which overlays infinite embodiment with a specific interpretation, namely, that the nature of infinite change makes a difference to our values even as that difference cannot be measured in terms of openness or closure. The answer to the question will therefore vary depending upon what is being emphasized: metaphysical foundations or conceptual insights.

In what sense is change infinite?

There are many answers to this question, of course, but each one begins with the premise that change cannot be restricted by permanent limits. Whatever limits do exist are permeable and therefore prone to being overturned, precisely because they themselves are a manifestation of change. In this way change is infinite in the sense that it is continuous in all directions, spatially and temporally.

And what of death?

Although change and death are interrelated, they are not infinite in the same sense. The first is limitless because its existence has no permanent boundaries, whereas the second has no existence at all. Insofar as death is pure nothingness, it does away with all shape and form. So in the second sense of limitlessness what is intended has more to do with the absence of boundaries than with their porousness.

Don't these universalizing definitions of change and death ignore the diverse realities of social interpretation?

The fact that there is something irreducible in our experience of change and death does not in itself negate the relevance of social interpretation. The argument apropos of infinity is that it cannot be confined by any limits. If this argument is justified, then it does not matter if those limits are physical, social, or intellectual: in all cases what is finite is overturned and ultimately destroyed by what is perpetually changing. But how that change is experienced will of course depend upon the particulars of socialization, which necessarily adds nuance and distinction to what is otherwise a universal phenomenon.

How is infinity related to nonidentity?

In both cases of infinity, the same is pervaded by the other. If there are no fixed boundaries or limits, then what is inside is perpetually exposed to what is outside. We are not isolated in detached, self-enclosed worlds of solipsism. And since life always experiences itself as finite and vanishing, whatever is experienced in the moment always includes something from outside of that moment. As long as change is continuous it is impossible to experience any particular moment as a purely self-identical phenomenon. Nonidentity is therefore the primordial condition of both life and reality as overflowing themselves into that which is open, exuberant, and measureless.

When it is argued that death is inherently meaningless, doesn't this overlook the meaning that we give to it from a variety of cultural perspectives?

It is true that death will always have a certain meaning given a specific cultural approach to it. So what is meaningless does not do away with this fact. But it does imply that whatever meaning is ascribed to it will ultimately be overturned and transformed into nothingness. The inherent aspect of meaninglessness thus points to this asymmetrical relationship in which all value and meaning inevitably disappear.

This argument presupposes a tragic outlook in which meaning perpetually slips away from itself and is ultimately vanquished by meaninglessness. But if we refrain from investing in the construction of values, which are themselves temporary, then isn't it possible to avoid the sense of personal loss that comes with their demise?

The religious and philosophical traditions which emphasize non-possessiveness are right that tragedy is necessarily associated with our attachments: if we are attached to someone or something then we feel pain when that attachment is dissolved. And since all attachments are temporary, they will always bring about the tragedy of pain, suffering, and dissolution. But it is difficult to deny that social and linguistic creatures such as ourselves have values which are in some way or another invested in life. There is no privileged position from which we could identify with pure oneness or emptiness. So if we have any values at all, which seems reasonable to say for the vast majority of us, then those values will be attached to the real world of change which necessarily brings about the destruction of those values.

In the previous response it is suggested that we cannot identify with pure emptiness, yet the concept and argument derived from entropic affirmation seems to imply just the opposite, namely, that we are always invested in the pure emptiness and nothingness of death. Isn't this a contradiction?

The difference here is that in the latter case the identification with emptiness takes place from a limited, fragile, and tragic perspective. Entropic affirmation does imply that our values are pervaded with absence, in particular the absence that is associated with mortality, but this relationship is simply the condition of life understood as temporary, impure, and embodied. This may be a contradiction of sorts, but it is implicit in everything we do and thus cannot be avoided. By contrast, the presupposition that we can identify with emptiness in a way that transcends suffering or loss is a contradiction that cannot be actualized at all: the only affirmation of emptiness that takes place is by way of the emptiness of something that exists in the world of change that inevitably destroys the existence of all things.

If it is true that life is finite and mortal, doesn't that preclude it from the experience of anything infinite?

To the contrary, since there is no sharp distinction between the inside and the outside, the self and the other, what is infinitely changing pervades finite boundaries. If the infinite were restricted to the outside, then by definition it would no longer be infinite. So the paradox of human embodiment (which is infinite embodiment) is that we experience the infinite from a finite, particular perspective.

Why the desire to associate change with otherness, heterogeneity, the real, the impossible, and other such terms? Doesn't this involve a misappropriation on some level?

There are many reasons, from the historical to the theoretical, to make these associations. In the main, insofar as what is continuously changing and nonidentical resists being assimilated into finite systems of language, culture, or politics, it does not seem unreasonable to think of it as radically other. It is exactly that which is irreducible to the same and the homogenous. Likewise for the impossible: if the contingency of change has no rational starting point, as with a prime mover, then its reality exceeds human categories of explanation in terms of what makes logical sense. It is real but impossible. And so on.

According to entropic affirmation, all values affirm the infinity of change and death (and do so equally), but how is this possible if those values are infinitely exceeded by what they value?

As stated above, there is no absolute dichotomy between the finite and the infinite. So while it is true that infinite change exceeds all values equally, that does not imply that they themselves remain immune to its fluctuating circumstances. If it remained fully outside of their range, it would not be truly infinite. Hence they affirm it, but since they are finite their affirmation always falls short, which is to say that they never fully encompass, control, or subordinate what is thereby affirmed. In this way it is possible to affirm that which exceeds the affirmation, since the affirmation is itself traversed by that same infinite excess.

The above answer fails insofar as some values reject the reality of death and nothingness. Why argue that all values affirm death (or strangeness, the abyss, the impossible, etc.) when there are so many examples to the contrary?

Entropic affirmation does not argue against either the rejection or denial of death. What is stated is that all values affirm it equally, not that they affirm it without any reservation at all. Indeed, it is impossible to affirm nothingness without some mode of denial or distance, for the very reason that what is limitless can never be contained within the parameters of moral and cultural affirmation. There is always immersion in the infinite as well as denial and repression; one cannot exist without the other. But what applies to the first also applies to the second, which is to say that modes of denial are always equal for the same reasons that have been provided in the context of affirmation—for there can be no degrees of difference in relation to that which exceeds all measurement.

What of particular forms of denial and repression? Couldn't it be said that there are certain events that are repressed more than others?

That is correct since there is a difference between pure nothingness and its embodiment. So while it is impossible to say which values are more or less open to death, as they are equally open to it, the caveat must be added that specific forms of embodiment are not of the same order. For example, it is quite likely that I repress a traumatic event in my past more than a pleasant one, even though both of these events are themselves equally open to what is absolutely and infinitely outside. The difference, then, has to do with relations: are we talking about relations with something absolutely outside, as with death, or in the sense of a comparison between particular events, memories, values, and so forth?

There appear to be different formulations of entropic affirmation in relation to change, death, infinity, groundlessness, contingency, and so on? Where is the consistency?

Given that each of the above concepts (as with change and death) are closely related, there are bound to be a variety of formulations of entropic affirmation. The reason why it is said, for example, that all values affirm death equally is because, as stated earlier, it is a form of infinity or limitlessness. That which exceeds all measurement cannot be the standard by which values are distinguished. And this is the same argument that is made in reference to change, albeit in reference to permeable boundaries rather than their pure and absolute absence. Moreover, if the abyss of change and temporality does away with the metaphysical presumption of necessity, then, by way of another formulation, it can be inferred that all things embody the contingency of the world equally—at least insofar as they are all equally unnecessary.

Another formulation of entropic affirmation implies that all values affirm death as opposed to everlasting life. But aren't there clear counterexamples to this?

One such counterexample would include anyone who professes belief in the afterlife. Beliefs and values, however, do not always line up in a perfectly symmetrical fashion. So it is always possible for a belief to misrepresent one's values and desires. The argument from entropic affirmation implies that these values and desires embrace death insofar as they themselves cannot be separated from the change that annihilates them. It is not as if change and death only exist on the outside. To the contrary, these values are the embodiment of tendencies which make the values themselves self-destructive. In this way what is valued and affirmed cannot be separated from such self-destructive tendencies, regardless of what is said or professed in terms of beliefs.

If it is granted that the infinite (whether in relation to change, death, groundlessness, etc.) cannot serve as a means for distinguishing value systems, then why make reference to it at all?

The temptation, of course, is to infer that the infinite is irrelevant to our values. However, the argument of thanato-vitalism is that this inference is too quick. While it is true that we cannot distinguish our values on the basis of how open or responsive they are to infinite alterity, this does not imply that the latter loses all significance. The task of the present method is therefore to explore this significance in relation to a number of areas, especially in regard to agonistic pathos.

Doesn't entropic affirmation (and likewise thanato-vitalism) rely upon a straw man argument? It makes the critique that we cannot draw firm distinctions between openness and closure vis-à-vis change, death, or anything at all that infinitely exceeds social values. But who draws such firm distinctions? By most sophisticated accounts, openness to either nonidentity or the immeasurable is simply an ideal, one which is never fully attained and therefore necessarily implicates at least some degree of closure.

The argument of entropic affirmation is that there is no difference at all between openness and closure in relation to the infinite. All values are thus equally open to whatever can be described as limitless, as with change, death, and otherness. To say that there is no difference at all, then, is to formulate a critique not only of firm distinctions—but any distinctions whatsoever. The contention that values should hold up an ideal of infinite responsibility is therefore false. As long as all values equally attain this "ideal," precisely for the reason that it cannot be measured or defined, implies that it cannot help us identify which ones are more responsive to it than others.

Isn't it possible that we only affirm self-destructive processes of change because we have no choice in the matter? If life and death are bound together in everything that we do, then it should be acknowledged that we are constrained by this existential fact. Given a choice, it's more than conceivable that we would prefer the immortal and perfect life as opposed to the one that currently defines us.

It is true that we are constrained by the circumstances of the world, but it is precisely this fact that makes a choice what it is: something defined by its imperfect options. Insofar as the immortal life no longer has a need or desire for anything, it cannot be conceptualized in relation to such imperfections. It therefore transcends the world of choice, as that world is marked by time and incongruity. To say that I would prefer a life without imperfection, then, is to say that my preference is to do away with the very conditions which make my preference possible at all. This is obviously a contradiction.

It is no less of a contradiction than entropic affirmation, which likewise states that we desire the ineluctable destruction of everything that makes us who we are: contingent, temporal, and impossible.

The difference between the two alternatives is that one is a lived paradox while the other is not. When it comes to entropic affirmation, we simply cannot live in any other way except as temporal beings destined for permanent annihilation. This is a paradox in the sense that we carry absence within the presence of life, but it is a paradox entirely consistent with the nature of finite, lived values. By comparison, if we think of eternal life in its most complete sense, existing apart from any weakness whatsoever, then we have a contradiction that cannot be sustained for even a moment. The perfect and immortal life is not life but the absence of those conditions which make life livable. The imperfect life associated with entropic values, however, is not only livable but real and observable.

It is said that we affirm death in all of our values, but this fails to account for modes of ideology embraced for their powers of denial in the face of mortality, imperfection, the inhuman, and suchlike.

All of the arguments marshaled forth in favor of entropic affirmation should also be applied to various modes of denial and rejection: if that which is infinite must always be affirmed to the same degree in all of our values, then it must also be disavowed to the same degree. And just as we never completely affirm that which transcends us, neither do we completely reject it.

Is this only a quantitative argument?

Not at all. There is no inherent moral standard associated with either change or absence, so qualitative distinctions between values will be as incommensurable with infinity as quantitative ones.

What is the catastrophic trajectory?

It is the argument that when we disavow something irreducible—from radical otherness to the abyss and heterogeneity—certain catastrophic tendencies are likely to follow. The argument is made in a number of different ways, but there is always a link between the disavowal and such things as war, violence, self-destruction, scapegoating, environmental destruction, and so forth.

How is this trajectory related to the above concepts of change, death, and infinity?

I argue in this book that it is infinite embodiment which is the primary irreducible element in life. And insofar as entropic affirmation precludes greater or lesser rejections of this infinity, it follows that there is no catastrophic trajectory; the case typically made for it is invalid.

Doesn't this fly in the face of empirical evidence supporting such catastrophic tendencies?

There is no doubt at all that there is empirical evidence showing that certain societal norms and practices have unnecessarily destructive consequences. I fully agree with this. But this has nothing to do with how those norms and practices embody infinite change, death, or otherness.

Is this rejection of the trajectory nothing more than a reformulation of Habermas's?

I agree with Habermas that, for example, Bataille's distinction between unproductive and catastrophic expenditures does nothing for us in terms of making predictions. It is best to do away with this unproven hypothesis. But it shouldn't therefore be inferred that the concept of irreducible infinity is irrelevant to understanding social life. Whereas Habermas draws precisely this inference, I have tried to show instead that the affirmation of infinity orients our social values according to principles of entropic refraction and agonistic pathos. It seems to me that this makes the concept of entropic affirmation something more than a formulation describing how all values embody infinity equally, as it also implies a certain orientation of those values which cannot be explained or understood from a purely pragmatic perspective.

Doesn't the above critique only apply to those versions of the trajectory in which the mode of irreducibility in question is transcendent in some way? What if we follow Žižek in saying that the abyss of the real is entirely symbolic? What if the inhuman is the very core of subjectivity as opposed to something mystical beyond language and social relationships? And what if Butler is equally right in suggesting that what is irreducible is the apprehension of precarious life, an apprehension that reminds us of the equality of that life? Isn't it true that entropic affirmation is inapplicable to such positions?

It is true that I interpret change and death as being not only immanent to life but also transcendent, for otherwise they would be defined by strict limits and boundaries. Entropic affirmation assumes this to be true insofar as it is an affirmation of infinite embodiment. The latter concept, in other words, is embedded in the former. In this manner entropic affirmation is very much applicable to those theories which fail to make this assumption, as it exposes their fundamental premises as limited and false. On the other hand, if it is said that there is still something infinite apropos of the purely immanent and symbolic, in the sense that they proceed by means of perpetual displacements of language, then the critique that there are no greater or lesser forms of openness to this infinity remains exactly the same as it does with theories of change and alterity that exceed pure immanence—for in either case, whether it is transcendent becoming or symbolic becoming, what is infinite moves beyond all distinctions equally.

What is it exactly that is "limited and false" about the premise that irreducibility applies more to something within each of us, as with the apprehension of equality, rather than something akin to change?

It is in the very nature of irreducibility that its reality is primary and fundamental. The apprehension of anything, however, is not fundamental in this way. To the contrary, whatever it is that we apprehend is part of a more all-encompassing reality of change that reduces everything to complete nothingness.

Everything said up to this point assumes that change is real, infinite, and absolute, but if this assumption is incorrect the entire methodology falls apart.

True, but the assumption is at the very least a plausible one. It does seem, after all, that change is real: we observe it every day of our lives all around us. And beyond simple observation, if we proceed to ask ourselves whether any experience is absolutely one with itself, without any hidden mysteries, the honest answer should be absolutely not. Indeed, if there were only one such experience that could be admitted as incomplete and becoming that which it is not, as opposed to being purely self-identical, we would have discovered at least one instance of change—in the sense that the experience would not be frozen in time and thus fully transparent within our self-awareness, but to the contrary unfrozen and moving away from itself, thus making it an experience of changing circumstances.

But what if this experience is merely an illusion of change, not real in itself?

Even in that case the illusion is something rather than absolutely nothing. Whether or not the experience fully and accurately portrays some particular factual content in the world, if the experience is changing as opposed to remaining one with itself then we have discovered at least one example of real change.

One example of change is not much considering that the method under consideration here assumes that it extends in all directions without limit. What evidence is there for this?

The evidence is in the nature of change itself. The argument thus far is that we have at least one example of real change insofar as experience itself, or at least one experience, is nontransparent, implying that it is not fully and completely present to us in every way possible. This nontransparency in turn implies nonidentity since the fundamental reason why it is nontransparent is because of the fact that the presence of the moment is bound up with its own absence, which is another way of saying that it is disappearing or undergoing change and transformation. But if this right, then it is in the nature of change, at least in this instance, that it is nontransparent and nonidentical with itself. By definition, then, change is not confined by discrete limits: it overflows all such limits with which it comes into contact. And the logical culmination of this logic of overflowing change is that is continuous, ongoing, and limitless.

Perhaps, then, change is real and infinite, but this still doesn't mean that it brings about absolute loss.

If change were infinite in the positive sense of continual generation, without any disappearance or loss in the world, it would be difficult to explain why we have negative reactions to it in terms of pain, suffering, and melancholy. If the loss of the ego is in reality a merging of our own limited perspective with a larger network of forces that sustain everything, then there should be nothing in the process which would at any point be felt as true loss. The entire process would instead be perceived and felt as bringing us closer to more vibrant and life-sustaining energies. And when it is replied that the ego perceives this process as loss due to its attachment to things, this merely begs the question at hand: why would the ego ever perceive its loss of attachment as a loss when every moment of transition from the thing "lost" to merging with all of reality would be a moment of increasing strength and vibrancy?

If all values affirm the infinity and absoluteness of change equally, then isn't the relationship between ethics and metaphysics rendered inconsequential?

Several authors have made this claim since greater or lesser openness to what is infinite is something that, by definition, cannot be measured. But what needs to be considered is not only the relationship between the finite and the infinite—but also between values. So while it is true that values cannot be distinguished on the basis of entropic affirmation, it doesn't therefore follow that the latter has no relevance. Quite the opposite: insofar as all values seek their own dissolution it can no longer be accurately said that some of them fall into the category of instrumental bio-power. Social values do not only seek to expand themselves via control and domination, but also desire to be limited and countered vis-à-vis other values.

No regime of power achieves full mastery over its environment, so this is not the real threat of discipline, bio-power, or any other form of instrumental rationality.

That is a valid argument. But if the implication is that we should none-theless remain concerned with an excess amount of calculation, then there should be pushback. In relation to infinite change and absence, as already discussed above, there are no degrees of difference in terms of assimilation: considering all of the technological and societal developments throughout history, from hunting and gathering to the steam engine, electricity, and the internet, in every case the incalculable remains pervasive. If it is replied that the problem with excess calculation has less to do with something infinite than with the particulars of a specific social practice, then it is being admitted that the value of instrumental rationality varies. In itself it is neither good nor bad, but depends upon what is expected in a specific situation. The argument proving that global warming is real, for instance, could not be made without a wide variety of calculations. In such a case we should embrace the calculations for being rational, precise, and accurate.

Despite the distinction being made above between the specific and the general, aren't there clear cases of excess calculation in relation to the latter?

What is the drive to mastery except the attempt to dominate as much of nature as possible?

This seems intuitively correct, but it is not. If we return to the general sense of calculation, we need to remember that all values are self-destructive, which implies that they do not simply desire to dominate the world around them—they would also like to succumb to that world. This is the primary reason why it is preferable to transition from the language of discipline and bio-power to that of expansive singularities, as the latter acknowledges the self-destructive tendencies associated with all social values.

Perhaps there is something inherently destructive in our values, but why can't we separate what we affirm from the ontological conditions of that affirmation?

This can certainly be done with the finite elements of what we desire and affirm. For example, it may well be that I enjoy the caffeinated consequences of drinking espresso, but would like it even more if it weren't for the bitter taste. It therefore makes sense to say that I affirm some but not all aspects of espresso. But the difference between a particular quality or element of something and its inherently temporal condition is that the latter is an expression of infinite change and becoming. So it is of course possible to distinguish the particular qualities from one another in an attempt to say which ones are truly affirmed (as with the example above), but the same cannot be done vis-à-vis infinite change: whatever it is that is said to be desired is in every respect and on every level the embodiment of nonidentity and nothingness.

If all values affirm death equally, then what's the critique of other theoretical approaches? Doesn't it follow from entropic affirmation that every methodology fulfills its conditions?

If this were correct, then there would be no need to defend thanato-vitalism as distinctive. But, as stated above, there is a difference between values and knowledge: what is affirmed in the first case may not be acknowledged in the second. Hence the possibility of cognitive dissonance. So while every value affirms death equally, it needs to be added that an awareness of this will help us to guide that affirmation in terms of its consequences. And those consequences include the entropic refraction that follows in the wake of expansive singularities, for as long as we remain ignorant of its reality—which has to do with the creation of social tensions and conflicts—we are less able to guide and direct it.

And how is it guided in a beneficial way?

A complete answer to this answer requires a book in its own right, one which goes beyond the primarily methodological developments in this one. But the issue of scapegoating that was explored in Chapter 5 is pertinent here as it helps to distinguish necessary from self-defeating modes of entropic refraction. In all cases the process of refraction lends itself to the creation of social divisions, so in a general sense those divisions and tensions cannot be avoided. But what is true in a general sense doesn't therefore apply to all cases and situations, and in fact it is in our interest to be discerning. On the one hand, in some cases we will detect a certain amount of scapegoating, which by definition implies that the process of refraction is unnecessary and self-defeating. In those cases, it is best to identify the true source of a problem and engage it properly. On the other hand, a lack of awareness concerning the necessity of refraction in a general sense will lead us to the idealistic goal of trying to do away with it in every single instance. This approach tends to identify all such relationships between refraction and social divisions as examples of scapegoating, but if this is false then we risk redirecting our energy away from realistic problems to others that have no solution at all—as with the eradication of all social divisions.

If entropic refraction is inherently self-destructive, then in what sense are we able to distinguish its basic, overall tendencies from others labeled as scapegoating? In the above answer it was stated that there is something unnecessary and self-defeating about the scapegoating mechanism, but these qualities make it difficult to distinguish that mechanism from entropic refraction in general. One reason has to do with the fact that the latter has always been described in terms of expansive singularities which are themselves ultimately self-destructive and therefore self-defeating. And if this is always the case, in the way that has thus far been argued, then describing it as "unnecessary" in some situations also seems false.

It is true that all manifestations of entropic refraction are ultimately self-defeating, but what is counterproductive and self-defeating in one sense may not be in another. Existentially speaking, it has been the argument of this book that the life and death instincts are bound together in all of our values, which means that affirming those values will always put into effect their own destruction. It is in this sense that what is self-defeating is unavoidable and necessary. But we can also speak of irrational and counterproductive acts in terms of the expansive rather than the singular nature of our values. Since there is nothing about the infinity of change or the nothingness of death that provides us with specific moral guidance, this can only be discussed and thought about in terms of what is expansive. If I love my cats, for example, then it is possible to articulate a specific set of goals that help me to solidify and deepen that affection, such as feeding them, petting them, brushing their hair, and taking them to the veterinarian. If I do not do these things, then my actions are self-defeating in relation to the expansive quality of my own values. So it is not in fact inconsistent to say that we should resist self-destructive actions in one way while arguing that those actions are ineluctably self-destructive in another. And insofar as scapegoating is a self-destructive tendency in the first sense, it is precisely the kind of phenomenon that should be resisted on the grounds of embracing our values as opposed to undermining them.[1]

Haven't others drawn very similar inferences from our responses to death and otherness to the creation of agonistic social divisions? What does this methodology do that is any different?

First, it avoids the fallacy of assuming that this origin of conflict has anything to do with greater or lesser openness to what cannot be assimilated. And in comparison to those who likewise avoid this assumption, it nonetheless makes a case for the relevance of infinite otherness for understanding why we should do our best to solidify and expand our values without falling into traps of scapegoating. In this way the path from entropic affirmation to agonistic pathos is not one which replicates the same sequence of ideas that we have seen elsewhere. If it did, its usefulness would become immediately suspect.

NOTE

1. It should be added that solidifying them also includes changing and correcting them when necessary. I should not say, for example, that I am obligated to expand the value of scapegoating simply because that is what I happen to like or prefer. If my preference is self-defeating to the overall trajectory of my desires and needs, then it should be given up. And what I have tried to say about scapegoating is that by definition it is this kind of preference: one that makes a mistake in identifying the true source of a problem, and therefore proceeds in a way that is counterproductive to one's own interests.

Bibliography

Agamben, Giorgio. *Homo Sacer: Sovereign Power and Bare Life*. Translated by Daniel Heller-Roazen. Stanford, CA: Stanford University Press, 1998.

———. *"What Is an Apparatus?" and Other Essays*. Translated by Stefan Pedatella. Stanford, CA: Stanford University Press, 2009.

Badiou, Alain. *Ethics: An Essay on the Understanding of Evil*. Translated by Peter Hallward. London and New York: Verso, 2012.

———. *L'éthique: essai sur la conscience du mal*. Paris: Éditions Hatier, 1993.

Balibar, Etienne. "Derrida and the 'Aporia of the Community.'" *Philosophy Today* 53, no. Supplement (2009): 5–18.

Barthes, Roland. *Camera Lucida: Reflections on Photography*. Translated by Richard Howard. New York: Hill and Wang, 1981.

Bataille, Georges. *The Accursed Share: An Essay on General Economy: Consumption*. Translated by Robert Hurley. New York: Zone Books, 1988.

———. *Inner Experience*. Translated by Leslie Anne Boldt. Albany: State University of New York Press, 1988.

———. *L'expérience intérieure*. Paris: Éditions Gallimard, 1943.

———. *La part maudite: précédé de la notion de dépense*. Paris: Éditions de Minuit, 1967.

———. *Théorie de la religion*. Paris: Éditions Gallimard, 1974.

———. *Theory of Religion*. Translated by Robert Hurley. New York: Zone Books, 1989.

Baudrillard, Jean. *La transparence du mal: essai sur les phénomènes extrêmes*. Paris: Éditions Galilée, 1990.

———. *Screened Out*. Translated by Chris Turner. London and New York: Verso, 2002.

———. *Simulacra and Simulation*. Translated by Sheila Faria Glaser. Ann Arbor: University of Michigan Press, 1994.

———. *Simulacres et simulation*. Paris: Éditions Galilée, 1981.

————. *The Transparency of Evil: Essays on Extreme Phenomena*. Translated by James Benedict. London and New York: Verso, 1993.

————. *The Vital Illusion*. New York: Columbia University Press, 2000.

Becker, Ernest. *Escape from Evil*. New York: Free Press, 1975.

Bellmer, Hans. *Little Anatomy of the Physical Unconscious, or the Anatomy of the Image*. Translated by Jon Graham. Waterbury Center, VT: Dominion, 2004.

Braidotti, Rosi. *The Posthuman*. Cambridge and Malden, MA: Polity Press, 2013.

Butler, Judith. *Frames of War: When Is Life Grievable?* Pbk. ed. London and New York: Verso, 2010.

————. *Gender Trouble: Feminism and the Subversion of Identity*. New York: Routledge, 1999.

————. *Precarious Life: The Powers of Mourning and Violence*. London and New York: Verso, 2006.

Camus, Albert. *The Myth of Sisyphus, and Other Essays*. Translated by Justin O'Brien. New York: Knopf, 1955.

Chuang Tzu. *Chuang Tzu: Basic Writings*. Translated by Burton Watson. New York: Columbia University Press, 1996.

Critchley, Simon. *Infinitely Demanding: Ethics of Commitment, Politics of Resistance*. London and New York: Verso, 2007.

Derrida, Jacques. *The Beast and the Sovereign, Vol. II*. Translated by Geoff Bennington. Chicago: University of Chicago, 2011.

————. *De la grammatologie*. Paris: Éditions de Minuit, 1967.

————. *Donner la mort*. Paris: Éditions Galilée, 1999.

————. *The Gift of Death*. Translated by David Wills. Chicago: University of Chicago Press, 1995.

————. *L'écriture et la différence*. Paris: Éditions du Seuil, 1967.

————. *Of Grammatology*. Translated by Gayatri Chakravorty Spivak. Baltimore: Johns Hopkins University Press, 1976.

————. *On Cosmopolitanism and Forgiveness*. Translated by Mark Dooley and Michael Hughes. London and New York: Routledge, 2001.

————. *Paper Machine*. Translated by Rachel Bowlby. Stanford, CA: Stanford University Press, 2005.

————. *Psyche: Inventions of the Other*. Stanford, CA: Stanford University Press, 2007.

————. *Séminaire: La bête et le souverain: 2002–2003*. Paris: Éditions Galilée, 2010.

————. *Specters of Marx: The State of the Debt, the Work of Mourning, and the New International*. New York: Routledge, 1994.

————. *Spectres de Marx*. Paris: Galilée, 1993.

————. *Writing and Difference*. Translated by Alan Bass. Chicago: University of Chicago Press, 1978.

Derrida, Jacques, Maurizio Ferraris, Giacomo Donis, and David Webb. *A Taste for the Secret*. Translated by Giacomo Donis. Malden, MA: Polity, 2001.

Dilts, Andrew. "From 'Entrepreneur of the Self' to 'Care of the Self': Neo-Liberal Governmentality and Foucault's Ethics." *Foucault Studies*, no. 12 (2011): 130–46.

Dollimore, Jonathan. *Death, Desire, and Loss in Western Culture*. New York: Routledge, 1998.

Eagleton, Terry. *After Theory*. New York: Basic Books, 2003.

Foster, Hal. *Compulsive Beauty*. Cambridge, MA: MIT Press, 1993.

Foucault, Michel. *The Birth of Biopolitics: Lectures at the Collège de France, 1978–1979*. Translated by Graham Burchell. New York: Palgrave Macmillan, 2008.

———. *Discipline and Punish: The Birth of the Prison*. Translated by Alan Sheridan. New York: Vintage Books, 1995.

———. *Histoire de la sexualité: La volonté de savoir*. Paris: Editions Gallimard, 1976.

———. *The History of Sexuality: An Introduction*. Translated by Robert Hurley. New York: Vintage, 1990.

———. *Il faut défendre la société: Cours au Collège de France, 1975–1976*. Paris: Éditions Gallimard/Seuil, 1997.

———. *Language, Counter-Memory, Practice: Selected Essays and Interviews*. Translated by Donald F. Bouchard and Sherry Simon. Cornell University Press, 1980.

———. *Naissance de la Biopolitique: Cours au Collège de France, 1978–1979*. Paris: Éditions Gallimard/Seuil, 2004.

———. *Sécurité, territoire, population: cours au Collège de France, 1977–1978*. Paris: Éditions Gallimard, 2004.

———. *Security, Territory, Population: Lectures at the Collège de France, 1977–1978*. Translated by Graham Burchell. Basingstoke and New York: Palgrave Macmillan and République Française, 2007.

———. *Society Must Be Defended: Lectures at the Collège de France, 1975–1976*. Translated by David Macey. New York: Picador, 2003.

———. *Surveiller et punir: naissance de la prison*. Paris: Éditions Gallimard, 2014.

Fraser, Nancy. "Michel Foucault: A 'Young Conservative'"? In *Feminist Interpretations of Michel Foucault*, edited by Susan J. Hekman. Cambridge: Cambridge University Press, 1996.

Freud, Sigmund. *Beyond the Pleasure Principle*. Translated by James Strachey. New York: W. W. Norton & Company, 1961.

———. *The Uncanny*. Translated by David McLintock. New York: Penguin Books, 2003.

Fritsch, Matthias. "Antagonism and Democratic Citizenship (Schmitt, Mouffe, Derrida)." *Research in Phenomenology* 38, no. 2 (2008): 174–97.

Girard, René. *Le bouc émissaire*. Paris: B. Grasset, 1982.

———. *The Scapegoat*. Translated by Yvonne Freccero. Baltimore: Johns Hopkins University Press, 1986.

Grosz, Elizabeth A. *Space, Time, and Perversion: Essays on the Politics of Bodies*. London and New York: Routledge, 1995.

Habermas, Jürgen. *The Philosophical Discourse of Modernity: Twelve Lectures*. Translated by Frederick G. Lawrence. Cambridge, MA: MIT Press, 1987.

Heraclitus. *Fragments: The Collected Wisdom of Heraclitus*. Translated by Brooks Haxton. New York: Viking, 2001.

Herbrechter, Stefan. *Posthumanism: A Critical Analysis*. New York: Bloomsbury, 2013.

Hughes, Cheryl L. "The Primacy of Ethics: Hobbes and Levinas." *Continental Philosophy Review* 31, no. 1 (1998): 79–94.

Irigaray, Luce. *An Ethics of Sexual Difference*. Translated by Carolyn Burke. Ithaca, NY: Cornell University Press, 1993.

———. *Éthique de la différence sexuelle*. Paris: Éditions de Minuit, 1984.

———. *To Be Two*. Translated by Monique M. Rhodes. New York: Routledge, 2001.

———. *The Way of Love*. London; New York: Continuum, 2002.

Johnston, Adrian. *Žižek's Ontology: A Transcendental Materialist Theory of Subjectivity*. Evanston, IL: Northwestern University Press, 2008.

Kearney, Richard. *Strangers, Gods, and Monsters: Interpreting Otherness*. London and New York: Routledge, 2003.

Keeley, Lawrence H. *War before Civilization*. Oxford: Oxford University Press, 1996.

Keenan, Dennis King. *Death and Responsibility: The "Work" of Levinas*. Albany, NY: SUNY Press, 1999.

Kornfield, Jack, and Gil Fronsdal. *Teachings of the Buddha*. Boston: Shambhala, 2012.

Kurzweil, Ray. *How to Create a Mind: The Secret of Human Thought Revealed*. New York: Viking, 2012.

Lawlor, Leonard. *The Implications of Immanence: Toward a New Concept of Life*. New York: Fordham University Press, 2006.

Levinas, Emmanuel. *Autrement qu'etre, ou au-dela de l'essence*. The Hague: Nijhoff, 1978.

———. *Otherwise Than Being, or Beyond Essence*. Translated by Alphonso Lingis. Pittsburgh, PA: Duquesne University Press, 1998.

———. *Totalité et infini*. The Hague: Nijhoff, 1961.

———. *Totality and Infinity: An Essay on Exteriority*. Translated by Alphonso Lingis. Pittsburgh, PA: Duquesne University Press, 1969.

Levinas, Emmanuel, and Nidra Poller. *Humanism of the Other*. Champagne, IL: University of Illinois Press, 2003.

Lichtenstein, Therese. *Behind Closed Doors: The Art of Hans Bellmer*. Berkeley, CA: University of California Press, 2001.

Mansfield, Nick. "Refusing Defeatism: Derrida, Decision and Absolute Risk." *Social Semiotics* 16, no. 3 (2006): 473–83.

Michalski, Krzysztof. *The Flame of Eternity: An Interpretation of Nietzsche's Thought*. Princeton, NJ: Princeton University Press, 2012.

Miller, J. Hillis. *For Derrida*. New York: Fordham University Press, 2009.

Mouffe, Chantal. *The Democratic Paradox*. New York: Verso, 2000.

Nietzsche, Friedrich. *Twilight of the Idols and the Anti-Christ*. Translated by R. J. Hollingdale. New York: Penguin, 1888.

———. *The Will to Power*. Translated by Walter Kaufmann and R. J. Hollingdale. New York: Vintage, 2011.

Oliver, Kelly. *Witnessing: Beyond Recognition*. Minneapolis, MN: University of Minnesota Press, 2001.

Rabinow, Paul, and Nikolas Rose. "Biopower Today." *BioSocieties* 1, no. 2 (2006): 195–217.

Sandel, Michael J. *The Case against Perfection: Ethics in the Age of Genetic Engineering*. Cambridge, MA: Belknap Press of Harvard University Press, 2007.

Schroeder, Brian. *Altared Ground: Levinas, History, and Violence*. London: Routledge, 1996.

Simons, Jon. *Foucault and the Political*. London and New York: Routledge, 1995.

Spivak, Gayatri Chakravorty. *Nationalism and the Imagination*. London and New York: Seagull Books, 2010.

Stiegler, Bernard. *Decadence of Industrial Democracies*. Translated by Daniel Ross. Vol. I. Cambridge: Polity, 2011.

Taylor, Sue. *Hans Bellmer: The Anatomy of Anxiety*. Cambridge, MA: MIT Press, 2000.

Virilio, Paul. *City of Panic*. Translated by Julie Rose. Oxford and New York: Berg, 2005.

———. *Open Sky*. Translated by Julie Rose. New York: Verso, 1997.

Žižek, Slavoj. *In Defense of Lost Causes*. London and New York: Verso, 2008.

———. *The Puppet and the Dwarf: The Perverse Core of Christianity*. Cambridge, MA: MIT Press, 2003.

———. *Violence: Six Sideways Reflections*. New York: Picador, 2008.

Index

About the Author

Apple Zefelius Igrek is an assistant professor in the Philosophy Department at Oklahoma State University. His academic interests include continental philosophy, cultural and political theory, the philosophy of conflict and violence, and post-humanism. He has published in a number of journals including *International Studies in Philosophy* and *Colloquy*. Most recently, his essay "The Performative Space of Festival: From Bataille to Butler" appeared in *Space and Culture*. "Prosthetic Figures: The Wolf, the Marionette, the Specter" is forthcoming for *Environmental Philosophy*.